STOCKWELL DAY

HIS LIFE AND POLITICS

Claire Hoy

Stoddart

Published in 2000 by Stoddart Publishing Co. Limited
34 Lesmill Road, Toronto, Canada M3B 2T6
180 Varick Street, 9th Floor, New York, New York 10014

Distributed by:
General Distribution Services Ltd.
325 Humber College Blvd., Toronto, Ontario M9W 7C3
Tel. (416) 213-1919   Fax (416) 213-1917
Email cservice@genpub.com

04 03 02 01 00 1 2 3 4 5

Canadian Cataloguing in Publication Data available
from the National Library of Canada

ISBN 0-7737-6166-7

Cover Design: Bill Douglas @ The Bang
Text Design: Tannice Goddard

The Canada Council | Le Conseil des Arts
FOR THE ARTS | du Canada
SINCE 1957 | DEPUIS 1957

*We acknowledge for their financial support of our
publishing program the Canada Council, the Ontario Arts
Council, and the Government of Canada through the
Book Publishing Industry Development Program (BPIDP).*

Printed and bound in Canada

To Sally and my family.
What else really matters?

CONTENTS

—

PREFACE

—

Writing a book may at the best of times seem to be a lonely exercise, with the writer sitting at his computer for hours, days, and weeks on end, churning it out. But while there is a lot of that, the fact is that nobody writes a book, at least not a non-fiction book, without some help from other people. In my case, given less than two months from the start of the project until the manuscript had to be presented, it wouldn't have been possible without considerable assistance from a lot of people.

At Southam News, both Joan Walters and Moira Scott were lifesavers in allowing me to mine their electronic library. At Canadian Press, Scott White generously offered the same kind of assistance. In Red Deer, city historian Michael Dawe, a Liberal no less, provided me with an extraordinary amount of information spanning the entire career of Stockwell Day. I thank them all.

Old friends Don MacDonald at the *Halifax Chronicle-Herald,* Peter Stockland at the *Calgary Herald,* and Roy MacGregor at the *National Post* also chipped in with some critical news and notes from various regions of the country.

I want to thank my agent, Linda McKnight, for pursuing the project, and the publisher, Stoddart, for believing in it.

Then, of course, there is the subject himself, Stockwell Day, who managed to fit lengthy interviews into his hectic campaign schedule, thanks largely to the work of his communications director, Line Maheux, and Logan Day. Stockwell Day also loosened up his reluctant parents, brothers, and sisters, who were understandably nervous about discussing their family with a stranger, and I thank them for their help. In writing this book, I conducted more than 35 interviews, nearly all of them on the record, and I'm grateful to all those people as well.

However the race for leadership of the Canadian Alliance ends up, I hope you enjoy the book. There is no doubt that the events of the past few months detailed here have changed the face of Canadian politics.

Cheers and God bless,
Claire Hoy

Toronto
May 1, 2000

1

THE PITCH

—

"It's percolating. It's moving. We're onto something historic here."
— STOCKWELL DAY, APRIL 19, 2000 TORONTO

We'll see.

Everybody knows the scenario.

In the 1997 federal election, just as they had done in 1993, the Liberals owned mighty Ontario. With about 49 percent of the popular vote, they won 101 of the 103 seats, their perfect score broken only by Independent John Nunziata, a former Liberal, in Toronto, and by Tory Jim Jones in Markham, north of Toronto.

For all that, however, Prime Minister Jean Chrétien's comfortable 1993 majority shrank to a razor-thin majority of 155 seats in the 301-member House of Commons, down 22 seats. Do the math yourself. Had Reform won just five of those Ontario seats, the Liberals would have lost their majority.

But they couldn't do it. Preston Manning, Reform's founder and only leader, making his second attempt to break through in Ontario, rode his horse in from the West only to fall out of the saddle. He had fared better in his first try, without the "advantage" of four years in opposition.

Manning loves to boast that he won a million votes in Ontario in the last election. He didn't. The Tories, under the popular Jean Charest, did. But Manning dropped from almost one million in his inaugural effort to woo Ontarians in 1993 to 887,000 in 1997, a precipitous decline that cost Reform the only seat it has ever won in Ontario or, for that matter, anywhere east of Manitoba.

Even so, Reform still finished second in 40 ridings, often not far behind the winning Liberals. And in 29 Ontario ridings the combined Reform-Conservative vote surpassed the Liberals' winning margin, and came very close in a dozen more.

With Joe Clark and his dispirited federal Tories in free fall, the NDP apparently in extended hibernation, the Bloc Québécois still poised to bleed seats from the Liberals in Quebec, and, despite what you read in opinion polls, considerable dissatisfaction even among Liberals with Chrétien, things aren't likely to get much better for the Reform-cum-Canadian Alliance.

Not in Willowdale, however. Colour it red. The north Toronto riding is not one of those Ontario ridings up for grabs. It's granite Grit, period. Willowdale is the bailiwick of Liberal MP Jim Peterson, whose brother David is the former Ontario premier. Peterson easily won re-election in 1997, finishing nearly 18,000 votes ahead of high-profile Tory candidate Norm Gardner, a local councillor and head of the police services board, with Reform hopeful Peter Cobbold trailing another 3,000 behind, and the NDP barely registering.

Yet it was here in Liberal country that Stockwell Day came charging in on April 19. He drew some two hundred people to the Moonlight Ballroom on Bayview Avenue, in an upscale neighbourhood peppered with multimillion-dollar homes, professionally manicured lawns, sweeping driveways, plentiful parkland, and oceans of Cadillacs, Jaguars, and Mercedes-Benzes.

Day's organizers said they'd expected a hundred people. They doubled that. People came despite the fact that the meeting competed with the fourth game in the first round of the Stanley Cup playoffs between the hometown Toronto Maple Leafs and the Ottawa Senators. Toronto lost. Could this be an omen for Day's chances in Canada's largest city? Not likely. Even the most optimistic Alliance booster doesn't expect to win seats in Toronto. The point of this night, obviously, was not to convince the general public to rip up their Liberal Party memberships, but to convince the local Reform and Tory loyalists that a new party with the same old leader wouldn't be perceived as new. The meeting aimed to show that Day, unlike Tory backroom guru Tom Long — who has no electoral experience — or Manning — who has never been in government, is the only leadership candidate who has been able to put the right-of-centre rhetoric into legislative reality.

So the people came to see this western whirlwind they'd heard so much about. How did they know about the meeting in the first place? Day phoned them at home. Well, not exactly. But it was Day's voice they heard over their phones, happily introducing himself and inviting them to meet him at the Moonlight Ballroom. His message was dispatched through a sophisticated, U.S.-built, high-tech telephone system called Minute Poll, which allows Day to contact thousands of homes with a personalized recorded message.

A few days before the Toronto meeting, Day's team used the system to dial more than eight thousand Calgary homes, inviting them to a meeting at Calgary's Chinese Cultural Centre. More than five hundred people showed up.

Sean McKinsley, Day's deputy national campaign manager, told the *National Post*, "It really is a very effective tool. It is so sophisticated and it is incredible. It's akin to the candidate making ten thousand calls every 36 hours, which is physically impossible to do as a human being. Even though it's a recording, it really creates the impression that you're talking to Stockwell Day. You come away with the sense that Stockwell Day called you and he cares. And he does."

It also helps generate the impression the Day campaign wants to create: that their man is hip. He's young — well, youngish anyway. He's energetic. He's personable. He's a fresh face. And yes, mama, he not only smoked a toke, he inhaled. Who better to plug into the newest high-tech solution, eh?

Image helps, of course, and the charismatic Day has plenty to spare. But it's a two-edged sword. His social conservatism, while pretty much the norm in Red Deer, raises eyebrows — and ire — in parts of Ontario and to the east.

Substance counts too — at least, it doesn't hurt. And Day, with seven years in Alberta's cabinet, more than half of them as treasurer, can boast that as well.

Day is spending at least half his campaign time in Ontario.

"Obviously a good part of this exercise is to expand the Alliance into Ontario, and that's the key to getting seats," he said in an interview. "Everybody knows that because Preston won only the one seat the first time and none the second time, so people say — you know, I'm not asking you to knock Preston — but people say, 'Well, he was in but didn't do very well, and he actually did worse the second time, so maybe you could do better.'"

Why? Day, in the detached way that politicians have of speaking about themselves as if they were somebody else, replied, "I think the people of Ontario will tell me they like the track record. They convince their friends that they bring out to meetings, 'Here's this guy who's got government executive-level experience, and the things he's done are the same policies that the Canadian Alliance has. He has brought in legislation which requires paying off the debt at a certain rate. He's dealt with legislation that talks about having to have a balanced budget. He has actually brought in legislation which makes it illegal to have a certain tax unless people ask for it in a referendum.'

"So that's what people are telling me that they find attractive. And people tell me that I can communicate one-on-one or to a crowd in a way that there is a connection there. People look at my record and see I can work and build a consensus around a table and get the job done. People like the fact that I lived in Montreal, I can talk French, and I can listen to people in French when I'm in Quebec. People in Ontario like that."

The people at the Moonlight Ballroom seemed to like it.

Arriving half an hour late, Day and his wife Valorie, accompanied by Shania Twain music over the loudspeakers, slowly made their way up the middle aisle, stopping to shake hands, to hug, and to wave.

The introduction by Mike Heenan, a 27-year-old Ontario Tory organizer, and sales representative for a transportation company in the real world, went immediately to an issue perceived to be Day's major weakness in Ontario.

"I saw him speak and I liked what I saw," he told the crowd, "but I had some personal concerns with the leadership issue and the role of his religious convictions in that, and he looked me right in the eye and said he's never imposed his own values on anybody.

"Then somebody asked him a challenging question and the crowd booed," said Heenan. "But Stock told them not to do that. He said the Alliance is willing to listen, whatever your views, and that he's a great listener. But he also knows that you can't just listen, you've got to enact."

To warm but not overwhelming applause, Day, in shirtsleeves and tie, played the family card well. He told the crowd that Val, his wife of 29 years, and Logan, one of their three sons, were there, and that they also have two daughters-in-law and three grandchildren. He then slipped the hand-held microphone to Val.

"Thanks for letting me say a few words," she quipped. "He rarely does that." The crowd laughed, although Val's brief opening remarks are often part of the candidate's shtick. "I can just feel the warmth we have here in Ontario. Thank you all for making us so welcome. It's been an exciting life being married to Stock."

Then Day launched into a 30-minute history lesson on how Canadians have faced hardships throughout their history and have always risen to the occasion. Without any notes, as is his wont, and with barely an *um* or an *ah*, the candidate described his typical campaign day. It began with a business-oriented breakfast meeting, followed by a policy meeting, interviews with the local media, a luncheon speech, a coffee party in somebody's home, a host of phone calls, and an evening meeting. Then home again, home again, jiggity jig — and starting all over again the next day.

"It's a national past-time for Canadians to be critical of what's happening at the government level," he said. "But over the past three years, the level of concern has been increasing. It's more than just grumbling. The concerns are more profound and they're coming from people right across the country. But there's not just a sense of depression. There is a growing sense of optimism that something could be done."

That something, he hopes, is to throw the dreaded Liberals out.

Day talked about how the original European settlers had to learn from the Native people how to cope with winter; how we built a confederation when the differences seemed insurmountable; how we built a railway to the West Coast "when nobody thought we could"; how a country of eight million people sent 675,000 people "to face down the forces of tyranny" in World War I; how we survived the Great Depression and became renowned during the Second World War, not just on the battlefield but in the world of manufacturing as well; and how as a "little country of 20 million in the 1950s and 1960s, we showed how we can compete against the mighty United States."

But then, he said, governments began building up debt, "buying into the whole concept of deficit financing, which," he quipped, "just happened to tie into the beginning of a politician named Pierre. We've seen this process grow in Ottawa — a system that is not responsive to taxpayers and not responsive to democracy. We have a debt of $577 billion and the servicing costs at $42 to 45 billion, just to service it, not to reduce it.

"At first there was a vague concern among Canadians, and then an increasing concern. There was growing unrest with the justice system. People don't feel the same sense of security on our streets. And there are concerns over democracy, where our MPs are constantly strangled in their ability to speak for us.

"But again that famous Canadian resolve, the ability to rise above it and get through the difficulties, began to assert itself. We saw this at the Winds of Change conference three years ago. We felt at the time that we'd tapped into something, that Canadians had gone beyond the grumbling and were starting to get that fervour."

And all of that, he said, led to first the United Alternative conference, the referendum by Reformers on whether to disband the party — approved by 91 percent of those who voted, and finally, the birth of the Canadian Alliance and the current leadership race.

"We're hearing the same things in Ontario as we're hearing in Alberta. People are phoning the Alliance and walking in off the street. We sold 40 memberships in Brampton [Ontario] today to people who had never had memberships before. That may not sound like a lot, but it's happening in every community across Canada. A significant number of them are federal Conservatives . . . We're going to change the landscape of this country. It's percolating. It's moving. We're onto something historic here." Day said that, to sign on as leader of the Alliance, "you have to accept what you, the people, have approved as party policy. What a concept! Imagine, letting the people decide!

"We know that history shows the Liberals will say whatever they have to say to get elected. In 1968 Pierre Trudeau promised the Just Society, and right after that we got the War Measures Act. Then [Tory leader] Bob Stanfield said we needed wage and price controls, but the Liberals railed against it . . . and after they got in, we got wage and price controls.

"My friend Joe Clark — and I say that because he is my friend — had a little problem with taxes [in 1979] and put an 18-cent-per-gallon tax on gasoline. The Liberals railed against that too, but after the election they changed into litres, and 10 cents a litre sounded better than 18 cents a gallon. Free trade was a good idea, but the Liberals said no . . . they campaigned against it . . . but they got elected and signed the deal . . . and the GST — another flip, another change.

"We've done a disservice to conservative-thinking people in the last decade. We've caused that vote to split," he said. "Because of this the Liberals know that they've been able to get away with disrespect for the people and for democracy."

In response, says Day, the Alliance has a "positive, optimistic, solution-based, 75-point program" to turn the country around, leading off with lower taxes, which, he says, "makes people happy. You've tried it here in Ontario and it works. . . . In the last ten years in the U.S., real after-tax income went up 18 percent. In Canada, it went down 2 percent. If you feel like the wheels are spinning, in fact they are." Day said that the top marginal Canadian tax rate, "at which you begin to be punished for being hard-working, educated, and successful," is between $65,000 and $71,000. "In the U.S., you can earn $275,000 before you hit the highest rate. That's $400,000 Canadian. . . . That whining sound you hear is the sound of U-Haul trailers loading up and leaving the country because of high taxation.

"How many of you did your taxes? Did you do a little dance of joy when you sent it in? 'Yippee, I'm paid up!' . . . Patriotism is wonderful, but if you can no longer afford it, you'll say, 'I'll put the flag in my pocket and put it on the wall in my new house in Denver and sing "O Canada" there.'"

All of this led into Day's pitch for the Alliance's 17% single-rate tax, similar to the 11% flat tax that Day legislated in Alberta. He says the key is to "look after the poor first" and increase exemptions for children, so that parents can choose whether to stay home and raise the children or go outside the house to work.

Then it was on to his call for Canada to "join the rest of the world who have an elected Senate," and his oft-stated concerns for "another situation where non-elected people have the ability to write in legislation," that is, the judiciary. "In all fairness, the judges warned us. They said we'd have judge-made law . . . but there has been a blurring of the lines of democracy, a rising concern and some disrespect for the judiciary. A growing number of people want legislation to tell judges what to do. That should not happen. The judiciary has to be free of political interference. But we need to draw clear lines between the legislatures and the courts."

Day wrapped up his spiel by criticizing the courts for striking down laws against child pornography. "When the government of the land will not protect the children from the predators of the land, I think that government loses the right to govern the land," he said, drawing many a "hear! hear!" and his loudest applause of the night.

"There's a big rush to force farmers and other law-abiding citizens to register their shotguns and other firearms," he said. "How about a registry for pedophiles? How about pushing a little harder on that?" This sparked a standing ovation.

The first question was on the national debt. Day says the Liberal plan will take 191 years to pay it down, while the Alliance would do it in 50 years and save $3.5 trillion in interest. Then came a query on the flat tax. Then it was health care, specifically on how Day feels about Alberta's controversial Bill 11 health reform. He supports it, saying that all Alberta wants is to set up facilities such as "the Shouldice Clinic just up the road from here. . . . The questions to ask are: Will it result in smaller lineups? Will it mean greater access to service? Will it mean better care with nobody being charged for the service? . . . We need to find a better way to serve the public, but within the [Canada] Health Act. . . . In every other area we know of, if you specialize in certain activities you can bring service in at a lower price. There's no reason that can't apply to health care as well . . . just as long as you meet all the requirements of the [Canada Health] act."

After a few more questions on the Wheat Board, Senate reform, and more on the deficit — but none on Day's controversial social-conservative views on abortion, capital punishment, or homosexuality — Day thanked everybody and left.

That night, the Alliance sold eight new memberships. The earth hadn't moved, but Day had staked out his ground and headed off for his next three days in Ontario.

⁓

Ramesh Rajaratnam, a 51-year-old with a small business and three teenage children, is not an unusual Ontario voter. In the 1993 and 1997 federal elections, he voted Liberal. In the past two provincial elections, he voted Tory. He showed up after a neighbour told him about the meeting.

"I had some worries about these people [Alliance]," he said, "so I thought I'd see for myself."

Did he like what he saw? "Yes, particularly his emphasis on the family, his relationship with his wife, and his acknowledgement [in a post-speech scrum] about the importance of immigration. That's not the sort of thing we've heard about the Alliance."

Was he buying an Alliance membership? "Not tonight. But I might."

Will he vote Alliance? "I might. But before tonight I would have said, definitely, no." In politics, that's considered progress.

"It's why we do what we do," Day said in a subsequent interview. "We're like that famous investment firm: we win our votes the old-fashioned way, one step at a time."

So many steps. So little time.

2

THE MERCHANDISING BRAT

—

The first time Day realized that he could make things happen by using his formidable verbal skills to stir up a crowd was as a 16-year-old student at Westmount High School in Montreal.

Naturally, it had to do with girls.

At the time, Day was active on the school track team, specializing in the 880 and the mile, but it was as goalie for the soccer team that he'd won the MVP award.

Montreal during the mid 1960s featured a broad cross-section of ethnic groups — Italians, Hungarians, South Americans — clustered in a variety of downtown neighbourhoods where the people took their soccer seriously. While neighbourhood schools were, of course, open to everybody who lived nearby, the concentrations of the various ethnic groups were reflected in the make-up of their local school soccer teams. Westmount, which was much less ethnically diverse, wasn't exactly a soccer powerhouse.

One day, after a particularly gruelling game, Day and his teammates were grousing, not about how good their opponents had been, but about the fact that the school always sent its cheerleaders to the football games, while the soccer team did not enjoy that privilege.

"The thing that bothered us about soccer, for those of us who played, was that we felt you had to be in better shape to play soccer than to play football," says Day. "And yet you'd never get the cheerleaders to come to soccer games. Football and cheerleaders were always associated with each other. And also with the girls — we had a hard time getting lots of girls out to our soccer games. They tended to gravitate toward football."

What to do? The team turned to Day, who, besides being the team leader, was never short of something to say, and asked him to get permission from school officials to address the issue at the next general assembly.

"So that was the first time I gave a speech to a large assembly, and I went up there without really thinking about what I was going to say. I can't remember in detail what I said, but I got the crowd engaged and I had them laughing pretty hard at times during my six-minute presentation.

"I tried to do this impassioned plea about soccer. And they concluded that we were right, that the football guys got the cheerleaders and all the girls coming out to their games. And our next game, for the first time in history, we had the football cheerleaders come out, and quite a crowd — girls included — which, of course, was our aim: to try to show the girls how eminently more manly the soccer players were than the football players.

"That showed me that if you've got an issue and if you feel strongly about it, there's a way of communicating it. Now that was the type of issue which got our focus as teenage boys in those days, but I've found that the same principle holds true no matter what the issue."

Stockwell Burt Day was born August 16, 1950, in Barrie, Ontario, the second of six children of Stockwell and Gwendolyn Day (née Gilbert), who were both admirers of influential American conservative writer Ayn Rand.

Both his parents had grown up in the Duplessis era in Quebec and were always actively involved in politics, encouraging their children to debate the issues of the day with them around the family dining-room table.

The Days had originally emigrated from Boston. Stockwell Senior (the name is an old family one handed down through the generations) and his two brothers were born and raised in Montreal. His maternal grandfather, Grant Hall, was at one time vice-president of operations for the Canadian Pacific Railway, and had a hotel named after him in Moose Jaw. (Years later, when Stockwell Senior decided to leave Montreal and move to Vancouver, the family would visit that hotel on their journey westward in a spiffy Westphalia van.) His paternal grandmother had christened two CPR ships of the Princess line, right after the First World War.

Day's mother's family had settled in the Eastern Townships, where Gwen was raised. Her father fought in the Royal Rifles in the Second World War, was taken prisoner in the fall of Hong Kong, and spent four tough years as a prisoner of war in Japan.

By the time Stockwell Junior was born, his father was rising through the ranks of the merchandising chain Zellers Inc. The company was expanding rapidly, opening stores across the country. When Stockwell Junior was two, the family headed off to New Glasgow, Nova Scotia, where his father would manage a Zellers store. This was followed by a stint in Fredericton, New Brunswick, and then they went on to Quebec City, finally landing in Montreal when Stockwell was five. By that time, he had a younger brother, Nick, along with two older sisters, to contend with.

"You've heard of army brats, kids who move a lot because their parents are in the army. Well, I was a merchandise brat. We moved because Dad worked at Zellers," he says.

When they first arrived in Montreal, the Day family lived in an upstairs apartment on a busy street in Notre-Dame-de-Grace (NDG), where Stockwell attended kindergarten and grade 1. Then they moved across the St. Lawrence River to the south-shore community of St. Lambert, where he stayed until they moved to Ottawa when he was 11 years old.

The first traumatic moment he remembers was being sent home from kindergarten. The somewhat distraught principal called his parents because at show-and-tell Stockwell had recited two short poems that the teacher considered unseemly.

He still remembers them. "We was down by the seashore / and I shall never forget it. / While she talked of love and other things / he picked his nose and et it." The other also focussed on nasal passages.

While he was nervous about being sent home from school, "there wasn't much my parents could say, since they knew I had learned those poems from my dad. His main concern was whether I had the cadence correctly. My mother said I ought not to tell poems like that at school, but they weren't upset about it."

This propensity for memorizing became a central feature in Day's life. At family dinners his parents and siblings would hold regular competitions, trying to outdo each other over who could memorize the longest and most complicated poems. Day memorized Edgar Allan Poe's *The Raven,* for example, when he was still in elementary school. He consistently speaks without notes, and on February 24 this year he astounded many observers by delivering his entire Alberta provincial budget speech without a single note.

When he told his mother the night before what he was going to do, she cautioned against it. She said that it was one thing to deliver a normal speech without notes, but with all those numbers in a budget, she asked, "What happens if you make a mistake?"

"I won't," he replied.

"And he didn't," his mother says.

His mother recalls one occasion when she and her sister were driving to the Eastern Townships to visit Day's grandmother. That was in the time before cars had seat belts, and there were four kids in the back. "Stock would have been about 7 and Nicholas, 4. The boys were being obnoxious, so I turned around and said, 'Please, I want you to sit down and act like little gentlemen.' Nicholas asked his brother, 'What's a little gentleman?' Stock replied immediately, 'Midgets.' It's probably not politically correct now, but it was funny at the time."

The incident demonstrated once again that Day is rarely at a loss for an answer to a question, whether he should be or not.

Growing up in St. Lambert in a comfortable middle-class home was a great experience. Day's father was constantly on the road and his mother relied heavily on Stockwell, as the oldest boy, to do chores around the house. But he still had lots of time to ride his bike with his friends and spend many happy hours hanging around the local swimming pool. He also joined the Cubs at the Anglican church in St. Lambert, finishing up years later as a Boy Scout in Ottawa.

Day fondly remembers the day his family attended the ceremony when Queen Elizabeth II officially opened the St. Lawrence Seaway, and periodically watches the home movies they took at the time. Another thing that stands out is the dreadful day in grade 3 when he first had braces installed on his teeth. "I was one of the first kids around to wear braces at that young age, so the physical pain of the first couple of days stands out pretty significantly. They were not seen as cool, at least not until I showed my friends that you could drag your feet across the carpet all the way across the living room, with the lights out, and hold a letter opener three inches from your braces, and sparks would jump right from my teeth to the letter opener. So I performed electric shows for my friends, thereby establishing for all time that braces in fact were cool."

In 1959, when he was 9, Day remembers the thrill of going to the Rainbow Meat Market at the end of his street, hockey stick in hand. He lined up with dozens of other kids so that Montreal Canadiens great Rocket Richard, who was there to promote the store, could shake their hands and autograph their sticks. "He had a black eye that particular day, which made him even more heroic in our eyes. It was a great thrill meeting him."

In 1994, with Day firmly ensconced in the Alberta cabinet and therefore on the stage at the opening of the Calgary Stampede, Rocket Richard was one of the dignitaries taking part in the ceremonies. "He got a great cheer and then he and his wife were brought to right behind where my wife and I were sitting. I turned around and said, 'Mr. Richard, do you remember the Rainbow Meat Market in 1959 with the hockey sticks?' So we had a good laugh on that. And it was still a thrill to meet him again almost 40 years later."

Leaving his friends behind in Montreal to move to Ottawa was a bit of a wrench. So too was shifting to the all-boy Ashbury College in the tony Rockcliffe area of the city, "with some of the incumbent abuse that goes with that. Not severe abuse, but the hierarchy is pretty rigid in that milieu." He adjusted quickly, however, becoming involved in both athletics and academics, and winning in junior high the Woods shield of merit, an award given to the best all-round student. A previous winner of that award was John Turner, a long-time Liberal cabinet minister and party leader and, for a short time in 1984, prime minister.

The family lived in lower Rockcliffe Park and Stockwell and his brother Nick were both day students at Ashbury. The private college was run on the old British system at the time. Day began there at level 3A, the equivalent of grade 7, and then moved on to transition, or grade 8. If you earned at least 85 percent in that year, you were allowed, with parental permission, to take grades 9 and 10 together, which is what Day did. If you got 85 percent in that year, you could move directly into grade 11 the following year, which is where he was when the family moved back to Montreal.

Day remembers his Ottawa years fondly. One good thing about it was that the Elmwood Academy, an all-girl private school, "was just 236 yards away from Ashbury. That was pretty memorable, what with all the fascination, excitement, and chemistry that goes with your early teens."

He played on the school hockey team — right defence, of course — and played goal in soccer and, "dare I admit it," was also on the school cricket team.

Although he describes himself as always having been "risk-adverse," Day's innate exuberance has frequently led him into difficult spots. An example is the time he was visiting his grandmother's house in the Eastern Townships, when he, Nick, and a few other friends were crossing a railway trestle high over a river. "We used to go down there against our parents' wishes and run across the trestle and drop stones down into the river. This day the Dayliner was coming; we could hear the sound of the whistle. My friends scattered, but I thought it would be really exciting to lie down sort of on the edge of this narrow trestle while the train went by.

"Well, it turned out to be a terrifying moment, because I hadn't counted on the force of the wind when the train went by, so I literally clung for my life at the outer edges of those wooden piers high above the river as the train rocketed by. Then I had to compose myself by the time I got to the end of the trestle, because I had to show my brother and my buddies that I wasn't scared at all. But I really was."

Another time, in an area in Ottawa called the sandpits (since redeveloped and turned into the beautiful Embassy Row), the Day brothers and two of their friends came upon a couple of kids from another neighbourhood who were swimming there. "We took their bikes and threw them deep into the water. There were two guys and four of us, so we thought the odds were okay."

What they hadn't counted on is that these kids had friends of their own. By the time the four had strolled around to the other side of the sandpits and sat down to chat, their victims had retrieved their bikes, pedalled back to their own neighbourhood, and returned with 15 buddies. "Before we realized what was happening, they circled us. That's when you develop some rapid debating skills and settle for them throwing our bikes in the water and a few punches to the head. One kid actually pulled a knife, and the sight of this actually terrified everybody. The other guys said he must be really stupid, so we all ended up sitting around talking about life in general."

Stockwell Senior says, "Politics was quite a dominant part of our lives for a long while." He adds that his eldest son "learned not to do dumb things," when, after legendary NDP leader Tommy Douglas lost his seat in Saskatchewan and contested a by-election in Nanaimo, B.C., Stockwell Senior was the "token" Social Credit candidate. "I was going to change the world once, too," he says. "But Nanaimo is not a good place to run against the NDP, particularly against Tommy Douglas. I lost my deposit."

Gwen says there was so much discussion about politics in the Day household that "the children didn't have a chance. They had to be interested in politics."

While they were living in Ottawa, Social Credit leader Robert Thompson decided to cross the floor and join the Tories. His children lived with the Days for several months while Thompson was looking for a house, so he was a frequent visitor. "Those were volatile times in Canadian politics," says Gwen Day. "It was interesting and certainly educational for Stock to hear Robert Thompson talking politics around our dinner table. He grew up in a rich time in Canadian politics."

His mother remembers one time after her youngest daughter Rebecca was born, when Stockwell, about 12 at the time, "had [Rebecca] sitting dawdling on his knee while he played chess with a friend. During those years and later [when they returned to Montreal] he was the one I relied on. Father was usually gone Monday to Friday [he was a Zellers regional supervisor by this time] and Stock was the eldest boy, so I relied on him a great deal to help out around the house. He was always good-humoured and had many friends and was keen to help in any way he could," she says.

In his last year at junior high, Day was chosen by the school staff as one of four hall monitors, equivalent to the high-school prefects. Monitors had the power to discipline kids who were talking in the lunch lineup or otherwise misbehaving. The main punishment was to "put them up to the wall," where the student would have to stand there, usually for

15 minutes, with his nose to the wall. "It was a bit scary. You weren't allowed to strike or discipline them in any other way, but you had to be judicious about the authority you did have, because once you got on the hockey rink or the baseball field, people could return in kind any unjust treatment that they thought you'd doled out."

During those years, Day became friends with David Berger, who later became a Liberal MP and then Canada's ambassador to Israel. Berger's father owned the Ottawa Rough Riders, so that meant getting to many football games and the thrill of meeting some of the players.

"We were friends. I remember Stocky as being a bright kid and fun to be with," says Berger. "I would describe him as popular. We did the kinds of things kids do, riding around the neighbourhood on our bikes, playing sports. I remember him as being a person who could rattle off jokes and stories one after the other. I remember when they moved back to Montreal I went to his home [on Montrose Avenue in upscale Westmount] and spent the weekend there."

Day and Berger also got involved in David's father's unsuccessful mayoralty bids in 1960 and 1962. "We kept somewhat in touch later on. When I was ambassador two years ago he wrote me a note to say his son Logan and his buddy Ezra Levant were coming to Israel, and he asked me to keep an eye on them and keep them out of trouble. Actually, I met them at a hotel in Jerusalem. At the time they were interested in getting Preston [Manning] to visit Israel. They thought he needed more foreign exposure or international experience. But it never happened."

When Day was in grade 8, Rough Rider quarterback Ron Lancaster (he got traded that year to the Saskatchewan Roughriders) taught phys. ed. at Ashbury. "Of course, when he asked us what we wanted to do for phys. ed., it was always football. He was our quarterback for both sides most of the time, so you could go home and tell your other buddies that you caught a pass from Ron Lancaster. It was a high-level thrill."

It was while he was living in Ottawa that Day first visited the House of Commons on a school trip. "I can remember wondering why all these people were allowed to yell at each other in their class, but we couldn't do that in our class."

He also has a vivid memory of standing on Parliament Hill as the Red Ensign was lowered for the last time and the new maple-leaf flag was raised. He could see John Diefenbaker standing beside Lester Pearson, and he could see tears on Diefenbaker's face.

"For a young person, you know, the emotion was one of elation, because somehow we were convinced that this was our flag and we should get all excited about it. But that was when it really hit me that this was a pretty emotional event for former generations. It gave me an understanding of what my father's feelings were for this former flag, as he was a world-war veteran.

"I remember the guy who was standing right next to us. It was quite crowded. We were really packed in there. He probably would have been in his late twenties, and as the new flag was going up this guy shouted, 'Go on John, look at it.' You know, he wouldn't look at it as the flag was going up. [The remark] struck me as disgusting and quite inappropriate. . . . He [Diefenbaker] was going through a pretty tough moment and it was unseemly to shout at him. I turned and called [the guy] a jerk. He stared at me but he seemed to quieten down.

"It was just a very interesting moment for me because I suddenly realized at that moment of time that maybe this older generation looked at things very differently, and that the time to change is also a time to sit back and reflect on what that change really means to people, both good and bad."

It wasn't long before the family was on the move again, this time back to Montreal and a cosy home in Westmount. It was about a 20-minute walk from the old Montreal Forum, where the 15-year-old Day and his friends would buy advance tickets for $3.50 and scalp them for $20.

"On game night you'd stand outside the Forum and invariably some young business-type would wheel up in a taxi with his girlfriend and hop out. He'd be dressed to the nines and pick up those tickets for $20 each without even batting an eyelash.

"So there were some entrepreneurial gains to be made, but still, you had to watch out. There were police who would stroll up and down, and scalping wasn't condoned. So you had to watch for the cab, watch for the police, then stroll around the corner and pretend you were looking through the crowd. Then you'd go quickly up to the cab, do the deal, and head down the street."

Day got into some trouble at a junior game at the Forum. He and his friends were lobbing water-filled balloons from the first level onto the fans from the other team, and he accidentally hit a security guard on the shoulder, splattering water all over him.

"I didn't think he'd seen me, but after the game I was walking through the parking lot and out of nowhere a guy comes up and gives me a shot to the side of the head. I sort of staggered and looked up and he was coming at me again. That's when I realized it was the security guard, so I took off. So my life was not totally without penalty."

Brother Nick, while nearly three years younger, was big for his age, so he got to hang around with Stock and his pals. "He was always the leader and the guy who called the shots, both in Ottawa and Montreal," says Nick, who is now a caregiver for disabled people in Victoria. "I was the guy going along.

"He was socially a mover and shaker. When he graduated from Westmount High he was king of the prom. They used to choose a king and queen in those days. He's always had charisma. He is easy to befriend and be befriended by and he's a faithful friend, always willing to stick up for his friends.

"I remember once when some guy two years older than me jumped on me for some reason and was roughing me up. Stock jumped on him, yanked him off, and let him know he didn't mess around with his brother. That sense of loyalty has been there all his life."

After his successful speech about the cheerleaders and the soccer team, Day was asked by the student council to make a speech on their behalf about student council nominations. "So I did the same sort of thing and I was saying the sort of things that were important to a whole bunch of people, and I got a good reaction, a standing ovation.

"Although even to this day there is always a little bit of anticipation just before the game starts, and I feel the same just before a speech starts; there's always a bit of positive apprehension. You sort of feel on edge just a bit and it gives you energy to deliver, whether you're playing a game or delivering a speech. That's something I learned in high school and it's served me well."

Most Sunday mornings, the Day family could be found in the great Anglican cathedral downtown. Day took his first communion at age 12. "It was very serious at the time." The next year he studied hard to memorize the questions and answers, the promises and commitments of the catechism, so he would be ready for his confirmation, a rite of passage in the Church.

"Two weeks before confirmation, my father sat me down. My father was agnostic at the time, although he did go to church because my mother was the believer. But regardless of what he felt personally, he would signal to us boys that this was somewhat important.

"So he sits me down and he says, 'Okay, you're taking these confirmation classes and you're preparing to make certain promises, but do you know what they mean?' So I rattled off a couple of them and said, 'Yeah, I've memorized them.' And he said, 'Well, do you know what they mean?'

"I told him, quoting from the catechism, 'I promise to renounce the devil and all his works, the pomps and vanity of the world.' So my father asked me again if I knew what it meant. I didn't know what a pomp was, let alone a vanity, which I thought was a sink, so I said to my dad, 'I don't have to know. I just have to memorize them.' And he said to me, 'Listen, you will be taking this promise in front of people and apparently in front of God, and if you don't know what it means, I'd say you've got a problem.' So he actually made me take confirmation classes again the next year. And I think I'm the first kid since Henry VIII that ever failed confirmation class. So there I was, now a 14-year-old, sitting in a class of nerdy 13-year-olds who had the view that this guy must really be a reprobate — he failed confirmation class."

Day didn't always take church seriously, however. Sometimes his parents couldn't make it to church but Stock and Nick would have to go anyway, catching the bus into downtown Montreal. "Of course, with our parents not there it was great, because as long as you got to the last five minutes or so of the sermon we could talk about it when we got back home. So on those occasions we would roam the streets of downtown Montreal. Everything would be locked up, but it was fascinating because there were lots of things to see. There were the usual street people that you'd almost get to know, and we would be fascinated by peering in the windows of the pawnshops and other stores, areas where we'd never be allowed to go otherwise."

That wasn't the only time Day decided to wander. One day his sister Deborah happened to be home when the phone rang. It was Westmount High School asking for Mrs. Day. Deborah, thinking quickly, said, "I'm sorry, my mother can't come to the phone. She has a heart condition. But if you tell me, I'll attend to it." So the woman from the school told her that her brother had missed his afternoon social studies class every day for the past week. Deborah promised to attend to it, which she did, of course, by holding it over her brother's head for several weeks, extorting things from him in exchange for her silence.

So where had he been? Well, the Alexis Nihon Plaza in the west end had just opened. Gwen Day explains that the plaza was "greeted with great excitement at the time. All those glistening new stores under one roof — it was the equivalent of the West Edmonton Mall or the new Eaton Centre in Toronto when they opened."

It turns out that the plaza, in addition to the normal goods and services, was offering live entertainment to its customers. "So Stock, seeing a microphone, was going there and doing a stand-up comedy routine. Needless to say, he stopped it after the phone call, but Deborah used the information against him for some time."

Day also spent a good chunk of the summers of 1965 and 1966, when he was 15 and 16, working at the McKay Centre for Deaf and Crippled Children, as it was called then, in the lake district southeast of Montreal. When he was nearly 17, just before the family picked up stakes and moved west, he began to emulate his parents, who usually worked on local, provincial, and federal political campaigns. It was the year that Pierre Trudeau entered federal politics, and Day worked for a long-forgotten Tory named Lambert. He lost. "But I learned something about the harsh realities of politics at the time. When you spend all your time hanging around the campaign headquarters, all the talk is positive. I should have been out following the candidate around, because on the night of the election the poor guy got whacked politically. Still, to me, there has always been a sense of almost second nature that the fact of politics is a reality of life."

And then it happened. One day, in the summer of 1967, Stockwell Senior called the family to the dining-room table. He told them that, while they all loved Quebec and they all loved Montreal, he was concerned about Quebec politics and skyrocketing taxes.

He had cashed in his bonus for $20,000, a lot of money at that time, and his Zellers cheque was $8,600. He was ready to go. "I left because it was not going to be a good place for our kids," says Stockwell Senior. "I just thought that there would be better opportunities in the West, and I was right."

"I remember we discussed it around the table," says Stockwell Junior. "My father said, 'Let's take a vote around the table and see who's in and who's out.' He did make a point that the vote may or may not have been the final decision, but he just wanted to know. We were all wound up and we all ended up voting that we were willing to make the move and go on to another adventure.

"It was tough on me. I had a lot of friends and girlfriends and I thought Montreal was one of the most wonderful cities in the world, with lots of excitement. That was a bit hard to swallow. Of all the moves, this was the toughest one."

3
—

GO WEST, YOUNG MAN
—

They left at the end of June 1967.

Day was just turning 17.

Stockwell Senior had bought a new Westphalia van — "I think I bought the first one off the boat" — for $3,900. He piled Deborah, Stockwell Junior, and Nicholas into the van, backed out of the driveway, turned west, and landed in Calgary five days later, after a side trip to Moose Jaw to visit the hotel named after his grandfather.

In Calgary they were joined by Mrs. Day and youngest daughter Rebecca, who had flown from Montreal. They hadn't left with the others because Gwen Day was recovering from gallbladder surgery.

After a brief stay in Calgary, the Day clan meandered even farther west, driving through the majestic Rockies and hitting Victoria three days later. When they arrived in Victoria, his father bought some property and subdivided it into lots. He also got into commercial fishing and several other business ventures.

The trip made a lasting impression on Stockwell Junior. "I remember very clearly driving into Calgary for the first time," he says, "going to the Calgary Stampede, and just sort of the brazen freshness and the sense of open skies and open hearts, and a level of friendliness that I had never seen before, on the streets everywhere we went.

"The next day we were all together again as a family and we drove through the mountains. I had never seen anything bigger than Mount Tremblant. There was this sense of overwhelming Western friendliness, the brashness and roughness of the rodeo, and the absolutely stunning grandeur of the Rocky Mountains.

"We had been there for about 24 hours and I was saying to myself, 'I am a Westerner.'"

The next summer, after turning 18, Stockwell Junior left home and struck out for some adventures of his own. He went first to Vancouver and then spent some time just kicking around British Columbia, travelling for a while, doing odd jobs, returning to Vancouver, then setting out again, until eventually he rented a basement apartment in English Bay for $60 a month.

"In those days, there was a lot of work around. You could take a casual construction job for three or four days and basically pay the rent and have enough food and money for half a month. Then you'd work for another three or four days."

It wasn't long, however, before the construction industry took a down-turn and Day found himself in long lineups looking for work. Trying to figure out where he could find a job without a lineup to contend with, he wandered down to the Vancouver city morgue, said he was interested in becoming a mortician some day, and asked if they had any jobs. They didn't, but the man he spoke to told him to call a friend of his who ran a company called Vancouver Hearse Hire. The firm had contracts with the various funeral homes in the city to pick up bodies from hospitals, the morgue, or the dead person's home.

As it happened, a regular employee was on temporary leave and Day got hired on a six-week contract. "He told me I'd know on my first pickup whether I was suitable for the job or not. We wore black suits and we drove around in this black station wagon with black smoked windows, and we'd place the insignia of whichever funeral home it was up in the window.

"My very first pickup was down at the city morgue. It was a classic John Doe, toe tag and all, and it was a welfare-case burial. But we had to take the client/customer to a funeral home for preparation.

"So it was just like in the movies. The city morgue is in the basement, with a big bank of refrigerator doors. You'd open the door and slide out the tray, and there's John Doe, an elderly citizen. In those days you had to bring your own sheet or blanket and you brought your own stretcher and we lifted the gentleman off the stretcher. I sort of took a breath because I'd never done anything like this before. The other guy had worked there for a quite a while, so he said, 'I'll take his head, you take his ankles. He's obviously dead weight and he'll be stiff as a board.'

"So I went to pick him up and actually some skin came off from his ankle. I jumped back, but the other guy, who was more adventurous, said, 'That's only skin slip, don't worry about it.' So I picked him up and of course all the cadavers were naked, and put him on the stretcher somewhat delicately, wrapped him in a sheet, fastened the two seat belts — one over the knees, the other over the chest — and we took him to the car.

"When I got in, the other guy looked at me and said, 'Are you all right?' I said yes, and I was okay for the rest of the day. . . . I got home that night in my little basement apartment and made myself some macaroni and cheese, then ran upstairs to get a newspaper, and by the time I came back my macaroni had gone cold. It was just as I was reading the paper and eating the cold macaroni that it reminded me of the cold ankle I'd picked up that morning. It was, well, eerie, but that was the only time it bothered me."

Other than that, Day loved the job. He worked shifts. On the night shift, he'd get to sleep in the company house. "You'd get a call at two o'clock in the morning and go out and do a pickup and deliver it to a funeral home. Again, it was like something straight out of a Peter Lorre movie. You'd go down some dark alley and a door would creak open and there would be the guy who worked in the funeral home, deep in the cover of night. I could see early on that it didn't particularly bother me, but it wasn't something I wanted to pursue for a career.

"Just seeing people on trays in the actual preparation room, getting shaved, for instance. Seeing people get their hair done, things like that. It gives you a different view of things."

When that gig ended, Day went back to a variety of short-term jobs, just enough to pay the rent, put food on the table, and have a little left over to travel around the province.

In early 1969 he moved back home to his family in Victoria and took some courses at the Institute of Adult Studies.

His youngest sister, Rebecca, remembers her big brother coming back home.

"He had learned to smoke by then. I remember being awestruck, peering through the heavy glass doors into the living room, how impressed I was seeing him standing up and leaning with one arm on the mantle smoking a DuMaurier. That was really impressive, and later on I smoked DuMauriers too." (She doesn't smoke now.)

For her, Day was her "big, friendly brother" who used to come home from Vancouver and do "loop-de-loops" with her. That's when someone grabs you by the waist and flips you in a clockwise fashion, much to the horror of watching parents. "And you know what? He's still my big, friendly brother."

Cigarettes weren't all he smoked at the time. These were the hippie years, and he and his friends were also drinking beer and smoking pot. On April 17 of this year, Day delivered a law-and-order speech — fittingly enough, to the Woodstock Chamber of Commerce — calling for stiffer penalties for drug merchants. *National Post* reporter Justine Hunter asked if he had smoked marijuana in his youth.

Typically candid, Day said, "I haven't for about 30 years but, yes, I have." And in an obvious reference to the pickle U.S. President Bill Clinton created for himself by claiming he didn't inhale, Day confessed, "I did inhale."

This admission made the front page of the *Globe and Mail,* with the headline, "I Did Inhale," over a large, colour, close-up picture of Day campaigning in Woodstock. The story focussed on the fact that "the former lay preacher known for his strait-laced lifestyle, firmly cemented his baby-boomer credentials yesterday when he admitted to smoking dope in his teens."

After the media scrum, Day telephoned his mother to warn her about the probable headlines. When I asked her if she knew he had smoked dope, Gwen at first feigned shock. "How would you think I'd feel, having just discovered her kid inhaled?" But then, still laughing, she added, "Of course I knew. What kind of a mother would I be if I didn't?"

By May 1969, Day and a friend had moved into a little cottage at Cadboro Bay, just a few miles up the coast from Victoria. The cottage was one of two in a nice residential setting, the last undeveloped lots in the area. (They've since been bulldozed.)

It was there that he bought his first car, a 1966 Plymouth, for $25. "I bought it because the radio worked really well, but just as soon as I bought it the government brought in the safety-testing rules and my car was ruled unfit to be on the public roads."

What to do? One day he noticed a newspaper ad selling chickens, so he bought three Leghorns for $1.50 each. "I thought we could use the car to raise the chickens and at least we'd get some eggs. I kept them in the back of the car and put up a bamboo curtain to keep them from going in the front.

"At night I would take the chickens for a walk through the neighbourhood and I used to tie shoelaces around their necks. I guess, when I look back, it must have been a scary sight to see some guy walking along with three chickens, but there were at least two eggs every morning, sometimes three.

"But some neighbour must not have appreciated what was happening with the property values, because some type of zoning officer dropped by and said the area wasn't zoned for poultry. I tried to say that they were my pets, but he wasn't buying that. So that night myself and my buddy ate the three chickens for dinner."

Around that time, much to the surprise — and ultimate delight — of everybody, Day's mother, Gwen, became pregnant. "I remember when she got pregnant with Matt, we all said to each other, 'Wow, they're still doing that.' It was kind of like the time when I was a kid of 12 or 13 and my friends said to me, 'Your father must be a sex maniac. He's done it four times.' I recoiled in horror at the thought."

While life was moving along on the home front, Day took a stab at university life, enrolling briefly at the University of Victoria. He studied everything from creative writing to oceanography, but he dropped out. In his typical, self-deprecating style he jokes, "I graduated very early, but they did not see fit to confer a degree upon me." He adds, "I took the view that I wasn't going to let school interfere with my education, so I left school and continued my education."

He travelled a lot, mostly in the U.S., going up and down the California coast. For a time he worked as a deckhand on a fishing boat. "It just seemed that life at that time was a series of travels and adventures, and that it was quite easy to survive if you wanted to work for a while and have fun for a while and then work for a while again."

And then he met the girl next door — literally.

In November 1970, Day was living in Victoria in a house with seven other guys, beside a house where three young women lived. One of them, Valorie Martin, groomed dogs for a living.

"She took one look at my long hair and dared to say that I needed grooming, too."

They were married in October 1971. Day landed a job in the computer section of the B.C. Department of Highways in Victoria. They lived cheaply and began to add to the modest nest egg Valorie had built up from her dog-grooming business. Soon there was enough to invest in a partnership with her father in the auction business in Kelowna.

The young couple moved to Kelowna in the spring of 1972. The first of their three sons, Logan, was born in June. Day plunged at full speed into the auction business, conducting weekly sales at the company storehouse, plus regular location sales.

"That got me back to working audiences," he says. "And it probably taught me more than any economic studies and made me a firm believer in the free-market system, because there is nothing more free-market than an auction. It's the establishment of value at that time and that place, not any higher or lower. Also, you learn how you can work the crowd so that you can get the best price for the customer."

They had borrowed from the bank to build up the business, and it caught on almost immediately, drawing large crowds and good sales. But early one morning, about a year after they'd opened, Day was getting ready to leave for work when he looked down the highway and noticed black billowing smoke. "I said to Val, 'It looks like some poor guy's business is burning down.' Seconds later, the phone rang and it was the RCMP telling me that it was my business which had just burned down.

"So that was one of those really traumatic times. It was the first time that something happened that I realized I had no control over. I remember rushing down there and running in and out of the burning building. With the help of some bystanders, we dragged out some of the customers' goods, which I felt wouldn't be insured in the fire. We kept it up until the police stopped us.

"I found out two things about human nature that day. One, there were people willing to run in and out of that front door with me, at some risk to themselves. Two, the police went around to the back door and caught a guy who was running away with some goods, with one of the customers chasing him across the field. So both sides of humanity were revealed. Some people were willing to help and one guy was willing to help himself."

The real trauma came later, when Day met with the insurance agent and discovered that the customers' goods had been covered after all, but all the things he'd put into the building — the construction, the expensive sound system — weren't insured. "It all literally went up in smoke because of some clause in the fine print which I hadn't read. It's an enduring lesson in taking the time to always read the fine print."

And so they were left with no business and a bank debt of about $10,000, a lot of money at a time when the minimum wage was $2 an hour. Day went to work for a competitor for a while. "We considered personal bankruptcy, but we couldn't justify that, because I felt that I signed on in good faith and had to repay the loan. So for the next two years I worked as an auctioneer and also took on other jobs to get this debt paid off."

One of the jobs he took for almost a year was as a logger near the Black Mountains alongside the Okanagan Valley, driving a skidder. "It was tough work; it was working with tough guys. But it was great, staying there and developing a real camaraderie with the other loggers. In those days they didn't have the kind of safety and occupational and health standards we do now, so there were lots of injuries. Every season there would be one or two guys killed by a tree falling on them or a skid rolling over."

Day describes a skidder as akin to a huge farm tractor, but it has a four-wheel drive and pivots in the middle. It has a thick cable on the back and six to ten smaller, choker cables coming off that, which are dropped on a trail of logs. The driver wraps the cables around the logs and winches them in. It's high-powered work and extremely dangerous. On his second day on the job, Day was driving too slowly; a more experienced skidder came down a steep hill, drove over his logs, and smashed into the back of his skidder.

"Skidders make a huge noise. They are just like screaming demons coming at you, and this guy is shaking his fist, and I realized that if I didn't get moving he was going to push me down the hill. So you learn quickly how to direct a skidder."

On the second-last day of the season, a friend of his, who was a feller — one of the men actually cutting down the trees with their chainsaws — was suddenly heard screaming in pain. "When I looked to where he was way out into the snow, he just sort of waved at me and fell over backwards." Day ran through the waist-deep snow — fellers had snowshoes, skidders didn't — to find that his friend had sliced right through his kneecap with the saw. He was covered in blood. "So, you know, things like that would happen, unfortunately, in those days, fairly regularly. So there was always a sense of 'you work together; you look out for each other and help each other out.'" The very next day a skidder was killed when a tree fell on him.

It was during that time that something significant was beginning to enter Day's personal life — God. He and Valorie began getting involved in volunteer work with the youth group at the local evangelistic centre.

Valorie had been raised in an evangelical faith. When she and Day had decided to get married, her parents asked if they wanted to get married in their church in Kelowna. "At first I said no," Stockwell recalls, "because I wanted to get married on a beach or on a mountain or up in a tree. That's where friends of mine were getting married. And also, I didn't want to give the sense that I was embracing any particular faith or religion. I was agnostic at the time.

"My view of the universe was that I had mastered my own destiny, was captain of my own ship, and I would be responsible for any shipwrecks. If these people were into religion, it was up to them. We'd sit around late at night and talk about why religion was a man-made creation to help people through tough times, that sort of thing.

"After a period of time I did say to Val's folks — I'd gotten to know them and enjoyed their company, and I thought too that it would make my parents feel better over the fact that I was getting married in a church — and I said as long as nobody thinks I'm embracing anybody's faith here, I don't mind getting married in a church.

"So the minister of their church [Paul Hawkes] took marriage quite seriously and would decide the number of premarital counselling sessions before he would marry anybody. I looked forward to those sessions. I said it was great that I was going to get a chance to sit down with this cloistered individual who had led a sheltered life inside the church, so, at the age of 21, I would be able to expand his ideas for him."

But a funny thing happened on the way to the altar. Day began to realize he was making a significant commitment and taking a significant oath. He began to reflect on his experience with confirmation in the Anglican Church and his father's lesson that if you're going to make commitments, you'd better mean them — and understand them.

Day describes Hawkes as a learned man who knew how to communicate. "He was willing to preach at the intellectual level and he got me seriously into studies of the Christian faith." At the same time, he and Val were expanding their circle of friends to include people who referred to themselves as Christians, people their own age who talked openly about having a relationship with God.

"At first, I found that somewhat amusing and then somewhat novel, and then as I got to know them more I saw they were talking from the point of view of something that was real in their lives. So the next several months I was doing some serious contemplating myself, you know, about the universe and the possibility that maybe the basic historical foundation of the Christian faith was true. I had always thought it was somewhat allegorical, even with Christ. I had never considered it in terms of its historicity.

"I had never really considered the fact that Jesus Christ did live as a historical figure. At the same time, I began to see him with his contemporaries. And the historical evidence as to the life and times of Jesus Christ and the things he said and did, how he lived and died, are equally as worthy, or more so, than the historical data related to the life and times of Julius Caesar.

"So that was the culmination of several months of a spiritual journey, and basically it led to both myself and Valorie, independently, but more or less at the same time, embracing the faith. So that's what happened through those several months. A journey of seeking, evaluating, and accepting the reality in terms of the Christian faith."

Day was getting deeply involved working with disadvantaged and dysfunctional families through the Evangel Assembly in Kelowna. They had camps for kids who couldn't afford to go to camp. Through their counselling work, the couple came to know people in Edmonton who were involved in an organization called Teen Challenge, an international, interdenominational youth organization. Before long, they were both offered jobs as youth counsellors. Their second son, Luke, was born in 1974 and then the family moved to Edmonton to work with street kids and kids who were on drugs, kicked out of their homes, or coming out of jail.

"It was very tiring work, but very gratifying. We were actually able to help some young kids get stabilized. In some cases, kids would return home, and in other cases, kids would get on their feet at school or pursue an education. We literally had up to six kids living with us. At one point we were living in a house and we made temporary bedroom facilities for them in the basement. There were nights when you'd be sitting up all night with a kid coming out of his heroin addiction and going through withdrawals."

There was also the time when one of the kids stole some luggage and all his wife's jewellery, but for the most part he found great satisfaction in the work. "That's affected my views on addressing the process, especially for people who take advantage of kids, heroin dealers. I saw first-hand the harm these people can do, and my sympathy level does not really run very high on the scale when it comes to the justice system and how these individuals are dealt with."

In 1976 their third son, Ben, was born. Now, with three kids and the remains of the bank debt still hanging over their heads, they decided to move on from the low-paying Teen Challenge job. Off they went to Inuvik, where Day got a job with Kaps Transport, an oil-and-gas-related transportation company. Day rented out equipment and maintained their large facility there. He'd outfit the crews who flew in from various oil operations and helped transport explosives out to the Beaufort Sea. "To me that was a whole new adventure. The Arctic is the last frontier, and it certainly was in those days. It was working in extreme conditions and was an invigorating situation.

"There would be nights — of course, in the winter it was all nights — you'd be driving out on the frozen Arctic or on the frozen delta carrying a payload of 100,000 pounds of explosives and the guy you travelled with was an Inuit worker, so you got to know a lot about Inuit life right from ice level up."

It was supposed to be a two-year contract, but Kaps sold out to Gemstar, so after just a year in the Arctic, the Days and their three sons headed back down south to Sylvan Lake, a small community just west of Red Deer. Day took a job working on the kill floor of Canada Packers, a job that required him to join the United Food and Commercial Workers International Union. In his first attempt at elected office, he was elected to the two-man union executive.

The meat-packing industry then wasn't automated the way it is now. Day describes the work as "nothing but blood and guts — hard, sweaty work. But I seemed to get along with the guys. This was southern Alberta, so it wasn't what you'd call strong union country. But the guys wanted somebody who would protect them, not just from the company, but from some of the union types that would come in from Toronto."

Day recalls one meeting with a clutch of union executives who had flown in from Toronto. "They had a very aggressive attitude against management. They were saying how you could make a point with management by looking at different ways of slowing down the operation, how you could get equipment to quit working, that sort of thing.

"This was a very defining moment, because I realized there was myself and one other guy, and all we wanted to do was to do a good job, work overtime when we could. Most of the men in that operation took pride in their quota levels, their productivity levels, and there was always a good competitive spirit to see if you could beat the productivity levels from the day before.

"A lot of those guys were raised in rural Alberta; they understood the agriculture community. Lots of them had been raised on farms, and Albertans have a pretty good work ethic. So there we were, sitting around with those big boys from Toronto who were flexing their muscles, and I looked at the guy beside me, a 22-year-old farm boy wearing a tank top and with biceps as big as my thighs, and he's looking at me, saying, 'I don't think so.' And I looked at the Toronto guys and said, 'I don't think so. We'll run this operation. We are not going to be stopping equipment. We're not going to be doing these kinds of things.' And my buddy next to me just kind of flexed his muscles a bit and I think they decided that they weren't going to get too far in this plant."

After a year in Sylvan Lake, Day and his family moved back to Edmonton, where he got a job doing contract sales for a commercial interior designer, installing drapery track systems in schools, hospitals, and auditoriums. It was 1977, and the first time he entered the Alberta legislative building was to install drapery tracks in a minister's office.

His work wasn't confined to Edmonton. Day got a contract installing curtain rods in the museum in Yellowknife as part of preparations for a visit by the Prince of Wales. It was an elaborate hanging system, with lots of curves and high-level work. Two years ago, when Day joined Alberta Premier Ralph Klein at the annual premiers' conference in Yellowknife, the group was touring the museum. "Everybody was looking at the artifacts, of course, but I'm going, 'Hey, check these tracks out. If you want to see some long-term fossil-like stuff, look, these tracks are still up.' I don't think they were as interested in the tracking system as I was."

Nor was Day interested in spending his career working on drapery tracks. Within a year he was packing his bags again, this time heading off on an adventure that was fraught with controversy and would ultimately propel him into the public eye and onto the political stage.

He moved to Bentley.

4

NEARER MY GOD TO THEE

I f you went searching for the buckle of the legendary Alberta Bible belt, chances are you'd settle on the town of Bentley, a community of less than a thousand people, close to a crystal-blue lake and a picturesque provincial park, about 40 kilometres northwest of Red Deer.

There are six churches along or close to 50th Avenue, the town's main street. Just up the street from an old hotel and tavern sits a pale yellow cement-block building that was originally a creamery. It had also been used as a pool hall and then a steam bath before becoming the home of the Bentley Christian Training Centre. The Bentley Christian Centre, the Pentecostal church that founded the school, sits directly across the road.

It was to Bentley that Stockwell Day came in 1978. After studying at Edmonton's Northwest Bible College, Day was offered a job as assistant pastor, doing youth work and setting up a committee to explore the possibility of opening a church school in the town.

Two years later they opened the school, with Day as its administrator. The Days stayed for seven years, until 1985, when Stockwell took a successful plunge into electoral politics, having failed at a previous attempt.

Day got his feet wet in the art of political persuasion as secretary-treasurer of the Alberta Association of Independent Church Schools (AAICS), a lobby organization representing 15 schools that were at that time unlicensed. He led a campaign, which ultimately succeeded, to convince the province to recognize church schools, and independent schools generally, as legitimate educational facilities.

But it wasn't just politicians and bureaucrats who had to be persuaded. There was a serious split within the AAICS itself. Some members felt that, since they were doing God's work, the government had no more right to poke its nose into their classrooms than it had to come into their churches and vet their sermons. They wanted no government involvement at all, including government funding. They saw their educational role as strictly church business. Others, Day included, felt the best way to receive formal provincial recognition was to invite school inspectors into their classrooms, so they could see for themselves that the curriculum was valid.

As spokesperson before a provincial committee studying the question in 1984, it was Day's job to put forward both points of view. He did, but unfortunately for Day, a published story on that struggle picked up just one side of his presentation. He is quoted in the story as saying that Christian private schools could operate without the permission of Education Minister David King because "God's law is clear. Standards of education are not set by government, but by God, the Bible, the home and the school. If we ask for [the education minister's] approval, we are recognizing his authority."

This is one of several of Day's arguments that have been picked up and widely reported during the current Alliance leadership race. They are used to illustrate the notion that Day's religious zeal would prompt him to impose God's law on everybody, if only he were given the chance.

In a recent interview, Day told me, "If you take two or three sentences out of a presentation, as some of those articles do, then it can be torqued into a pretty extreme position. I was speaking on behalf of the Christian schools then. It was my responsibility to present their position to the government, just as later on, when I entered government, it was my role to promote the public school system as well as the Catholic and independent schools.

"You know, there are universal principles which are embraced by most families, whether they are religious or not, even in this post-Christian era."

Day says that the split among various churches in his association at the time "was creating quite a problem. I was the facilitator between the churches and the government, trying to make sure that both sides could reconcile the situation. I told the churches, and some of them didn't like it, that if you've got a program of academic excellence that you're proud of, don't be afraid to let the people see it."

Indeed, in 1984 Day had done just that, inviting Earl Clark, assistant superintendent for the County of Lacombe school district, to inspect his school, but Clark refused, saying, "The school is illegal, and if we inspected, we would be recognizing it." Clark's criticisms weren't based entirely on academic standards, however. He complained to *Alberta Report* that Day's school took kids out of the public system, estimating the loss to that system at $50,000 a year. As to the legal question, Clark's charge that Day's school was illegal ignored the fact that Calgary fundamentalist pastor Larry Jones had recently been acquitted of charges under the School Act arising from his basement Christian school operation.

"Christian schools, of course, are motivated by Christ's standards, i.e., God's point of view," Day told me. "I was also trying to explain to the churches that people in government are mostly motivated by good intentions. The situation was coming close to a legal challenge. That's what we were trying to avoid, and the government eventually brought in a whole different classification to cover our schools. There was some sabre rattling at the time, but we found a way to make it satisfactory to both the churches and the government, to allow for peaceful coexistence, and I'm proud of my role in that process."

Not everybody sees it that way. In its April 13–19, 2000, edition, *NOW,* Toronto's weekly left-wing tabloid, which caters largely to the city's countercultural community, published a nasty attack by journalist Gordon Laird, focussing on Day's years in Bentley. Laird was not content with questioning Day's suitability for national political leadership because of his deeply held religious views, which, as in so many of the Canadian media, are presented as hateful and intolerant. Much of the article damns by insinuation, concentrating on the fact that Bentley was also home to notorious anti-Semite Jim Keegstra, the former Red Deer teacher fired in the early 1980s for teaching children about "the Jewish conspiracy."

The story cites how Day took his car to be fixed at Keegstra's garage, and that Keegstra attended a few of the 6 A.M. prayer meetings that Day held for local men. It points out that equally notorious neo-Nazis, such as Ernst Zundel, used to visit Keegstra there. If the implication is that the people of Bentley are Nazi sympathizers because Keegstra lives there, does that put Torontonians in the same category because Zundel lives in Toronto?

The article goes on to cite a report by former cabinet minister and recently retired Alberta senator Ron Ghitter, a Jew, that raised serious questions about what he saw as anti-Semitic teachings in some of the Christian schools. Ghitter, who was roundly criticized by Reform leader Preston Manning and others for accepting a patronage position in the Senate — abandoning his former position that senators should be elected — was careful not to accuse Day directly. "I would never make that allegation against Stockwell," he told *NOW.* "But built in that [religious] ideology is the roots of anti-Semitism. It's there in the roots of Social Credit — and it is in today's Alliance, though not necessarily in the leaders."

Ghitter also raised concerns about Accelerated Christian Education (ACE), a rigid curriculum developed by the Texas-based School of Tomorrow. Ghitter was concerned that some of the ACE material being taught in Alberta — although again, he didn't point the finger specifically at Day's school — was clearly anti-Semitic.

The ACE material was no doubt used in some of the Christian schools at the time, but Day said in 1985 that his school was never anti-Semitic or intolerant. "We refer to the Jews as the chosen people. The materials are against anti-Semitism."

Day's response to Ghitter's *Tolerance and Understanding* report was quoted in the 1984 *Alberta Report* article: "The Christian religion gives significance to all men. Jesus loves all people, all religions, all sinners. I do not want to see any law passed to limit anyone's freedom of religion or expression."

Indeed, even the *NOW* article — in the very last paragraph of the lengthy story, of course — quotes libertarian lawyer Gary Botting as saying, "Day didn't buy into Keegstra's anti-Semitic platform at all. Put it this way: if it had to be a Christian world — God help us — you'd want Day there."

But the article also quotes Gregory Rathjen, the current pastor of Day's church, saying that Day left behind a deeply divided community, a demoralized congregation that had shrunk by almost half, and $32,000 owing to creditors. According to the writer, "allegations of fraud were rife," although the story doesn't offer a single detail of these allegations.

Rathjen says that the church under Day "changed their bylaws so people would have no say — leaders appointed by other leaders, as determined by the Scripture. It was a haughty, arrogant, pride-filled story that led to disaster."

In other media reports, however, Reg Darnel, a former pastor at the Bentley Christian Centre and now a pastor in nearby Rimbey, has described Day as a bright, inspirational speaker, especially popular among young people because of his sense of humour and fun. "Stock is a man who lives by his principles, but not in a rigid, inhumane way. He was able to impart to kids the value in having a faith in Jesus Christ."

A March 25, 2000, feature in the *Toronto Star,* hardly a hotbed of Alliance support, begins with an illustration of the use of humour and fun that Darnel described as Day's method of getting his message across.

"Sitting on the knee of his wife, Valorie," wrote the *Star's* Daniel Girard, "he was the dummy in a ventriloquist act at an event welcoming new members into their church. She asked the questions. His lips moved, but her voice delivered the answers. The room dissolved into laughter.

"The sight of the assistant pastor playing the clown immediately put newcomers to Bentley Christian Centre, a Pentecostal flock, at ease. For those already familiar with Day's comedic antics, the routine showcased his humility, making the message of faith that followed more poignant."

Day loved school and church work, but in 1982, his appetite for politics whetted by his campaign for independent church schools, he took the plunge. With just over a week to go before the Conservative nomination for the Lacombe constituency, and egged on by people in his church, he joined five other candidates seeking the job. He lost on the third ballot.

"We had a campaign budget of a hundred dollars, which we used to buy some buttons," he said. "The night of the nomination we were in second place all the way. I hadn't dreamed for a minute that we could actually win; we just wanted to get involved and raise the issues that we thought were important. But as I walked away that night, I said to Val, 'We came in second and we didn't even try. Think what would have happened if we had worked at it.'"

The man who won the nomination, and went on to win the election, was crusty Conservative Ron Moore, a maverick business consultant who was ultimately responsible for making the bighorn sheep the official emblem of Alberta. He sat in the legislature until 1993, retiring after his wife died, just a month before the 1993 nomination. Some concerns about Day's religious fervour were evident during the nomination race, echoing the issue that has clung to Day throughout his political career.

"Some people were afraid that he would bring those fundamentalist Christian principles into politics, and they didn't want the churches running our political system," said one veteran local political observer, who didn't want to be named. "It hasn't proved to be true in Stock's case, but that doesn't stop people from worrying about it. You can see that in some of the media coverage he's getting in the current campaign. It may not be fair, but unless he renounces his religion, which he'd never do, then he's stuck with it. Every politician has a cross to bear. Stock bears his cross literally."

Moore says that Day as leader of the Alliance would be "a vast improvement over Preston [Manning]." Moore, who has known Manning since he graduated from university — and who did some work with both Manning and his father in the family business — says, "Preston has done a good job of organizing, but he has gone as far as he can go. Stock is ambitious, he's young; he always stood up for what is right and moral and for his principles. He isn't really a statesman, but he's a good politician."

According to Moore, Day has "certainly changed a lot" since that 1982 nomination contest. "He was a pastor in a fundamentalist church and he played the role of a pastor. He was more with the church then than he was a politician." When I asked him what he meant by saying Day played the pastor, Moore laughed and said, "That's a good question, but I think I'll just leave it at that. Yes, he organized the church people, but in that particular instance it didn't work out for him."

Besides Day and Moore, two county councillors, a mayor, and a farmer also sought the nomination, drawing well over 2,200 people to the Lacombe arena, a significant turnout for such a small community. Four years later, when Day did get elected in Red Deer, Moore got to know him in caucus. "He wasn't dynamic in caucus. He contributed, but he was just an average MLA. But in politics, opportunities come. If he hadn't been made treasurer, he wouldn't be where he is today. So, in some ways, it's the luck of the draw. But Day did a good job when he got the chance. You can't stand still in politics, you either go up or down. Look at Joe Clark.

He's had his day in the sun. I wish he'd get out of the sun. The country would be better off without him."

These were turbulent times in Alberta. The oil industry had suffered a drastic decline and most Albertans blamed the province's fiscal woes on Pierre Trudeau's hated National Energy Program (NEP). They claimed that Trudeau had imposed the NEP on Alberta, ignoring the fact that Premier Peter Lougheed had willingly signed on — a photo of Lougheed and Trudeau toasting the deal with champagne was widely distributed across the country. But the deal turned sour only when world oil prices collapsed because of the machinations of OPEC, the multinational oil-producing cartel.

In any event, Lougheed, who remains a revered figure in Alberta, had had enough of politics. In the fall of 1985 he decided to step down, sparking a hard-fought battle for his job. Day supported Don Getty, the eventual winner. He tried to get elected as a delegate to the leadership convention from Lacombe, but lost when one of the other candidates for the premier's job, Julian Koziak, swept the local delegate-selection process.

Undeterred, Day went searching for another political opportunity. It came in early 1986, when the provincial riding of Red Deer was split into two ridings, North and South, and Day decided to seize the moment.

Day had a problem, though: he didn't live in Red Deer. He knew several people there through his work with the church and the independent school movement, but he was facing the challenge of defeating two well-known local candidates.

Leaving Bentley "was like Montreal, the only other time I felt real sadness leaving," says Day. "We had a wonderful church — some great people — where we had great support. The school was going really well. We had started it with 30 students and it was up to 120 to grade 12."

This time he wasn't going to make the mistake he made in 1982. Calling himself an education consultant, Day moved his family to Red Deer. One of the first things he did was get a phone with the number 343-VOTE, the number he still has today. He used that phone to call about a thousand people on the Progressive Conservative Party membership list, many of whom had been signed up during the recent leadership process. He scheduled between three and six events each week: breakfasts, lunches, or evening coffee parties in people's homes. He had the PC list, the Chamber of Commerce list, lists of people he knew in the church movement, and another list of people he knew in the independent-school movement.

"I'd phone them and say, 'Hi, I'm having lunch at noon on Wednesday. Won't you join me?' If they said they were busy, I'd say, 'That's okay, how about a coffee party at so-and-so's house Thursday at seven, or breakfast Friday at eight?' It was an effective but low-budget campaign. Val made a lot of the lunches herself, the sandwiches and soup. We'd rent schoolrooms or use office space somebody donated. The whole campaign cost less than ten thousand dollars.

"It was all on the ground, a lot of one-on-one. We borrowed a motorhome from my brother-in-law and had large posters and balloons on it. I went to all the local events in it. Everywhere where people congregated, I was there with my festooned motorhome."

Day actually began his campaign, or had people begin it for him, several months before he moved to Red Deer. Duane Skaley, who ran Day's floor campaign on nomination night and had worked with him in the church-school movement, says, "We'd been working behind the scenes for months. He was interested in coming to Red Deer and we felt if we could get the support, he would move. Whenever people talked about his nomination they threw out terms like 'fundamentalist,' as if he didn't have any other support. The independent-school movement didn't just include fundamentalists, far from it."

Skaley, a member of the provincial Conservative Party board of directors, continues, "It was a real grassroots campaign, one vote at a time. That's still the way Stock works. He brought in a lot of people who were not Tories at the time. He brought in a lot of old Socreds, some disenfranchised Liberals; even some NDP supporters came over to him. It was our organization that did it. We got the people out. He was able to deliver the numbers that other people can't. He still can do that. People always bring up the question of his religion. They certainly did then. But just because you have a faith doesn't mean you should be excluded from politics, any more than you would be if you don't have a faith. A lot of people are not brought up in a church environment and don't know much about it. They see it portrayed on television sitcoms or something and they think that's what it is. There is a lot of fear more than anything else, fear of the unknown.

"Anyway, at that nomination meeting people from other churches were sitting across the aisle voting for other persons. Stock didn't get all the religious community votes. It wasn't as big a card as it's made out to be. You go to any meeting in this town and you're going to find a lot of religious people. That's just the way it is here.

"I hear people say, 'Why doesn't he keep his moral views to himself, just forget about that and get on with it?' Well, that's like saying Stock has strong views on a balanced budget, so he shouldn't say anything about that either. He has his views. Nobody's going to come back to him later and say they didn't know about it. But he knows that for most people at the door, the economic issues are the most important. That's why he talks about them all the time. But journalists, who have to write about some-thing, prefer to write about the other issues."

In the end, Day sold more than five hundred party memberships. He delivered an emotional campaign speech to the St. Patrick's Day crowd of eight hundred at the Italian Capri Centre, focussing on a revamped taxation system and a crackdown on pornography and violent crime. He also criticized the recent federal decision to allow homosexuals into combat units in the Armed Forces.

He won on the first ballot. He was 35 years old and headed for glory.

There was some resentment because Day was the new kid on the block who had parachuted into town just two months earlier, but there was also unease over the religious card. Ted Johnson, who finished third, said later that had there been a second ballot he would have thrown his support behind local park manager Jim Armet because he was worried about Day's "religious overtones" and his "heavy stance" on moral issues.

Ten days later, the local newspaper, the *Red Deer Advocate*, ran a story headlined, "Day's Religious-Politics Mix Irks Long-Time Tories." One of those was former Red Deer alderman and local Tory executive member the late Ron Dale, who had backed Armet. Dale said flat-out he wouldn't support Day in the election. "It's good to apply Christian principles to your political beliefs," he said, "but I don't think you should mix them." Another executive member, Jim Douglas, complained that Day got too much of his support from religious groups and "didn't deal with local issues." Gary Didrickson, then third vice-president of the association, said the local Conservatives were surprised and bewildered by Day's success. "He took us by storm."

The riding president, Bill Hull, who chaired the meeting, said after the nomination that the executive members didn't know much about Day but they wanted to meet with him to see if he had a "hidden agenda." They wanted to know if he was pushing his religious views or promoting local issues.

Hull, currently a Red Deer city councillor, is now one of Day's strongest supporters. "He [Day] brought an astounding amount of enthusiasm and hoopla to our normally staid nomination meeting. He had a lot of youth involved. Very high energy, which I suppose is like his personality," says Hull.

Shortly after the nomination, Hull invited Day for a "frank discussion" and bear-pit session with the 17-member Tory executive at, of all places, the Rocky Mountain Brewery. "A lot of us were concerned about him, but he readily agreed to come to the meeting and he made several specific commitments. He agreed to treat all constituents equally, that there would be no second-class citizens based on their religious leanings, that he would appeal to all sections of the community, the business community, our minorities, everybody. And he also agreed that he would support the public school system and would not involve himself any more in the private-school issue.

"We came out of that meeting and I think he garnered substantial support from the executive. There was such a thirst for knowledge about him at the time. He was very open and wanted to establish a relationship with us. He committed to certain things and he lived up to all those commitments. I felt much better afterwards."

Hull says he's not surprised that much of the national media initially focussed on Day's religious and moral views after he entered the Alliance race. "It's no different than what happened here. But we discussed it with him and he gave us the straight goods. Certainly his Christian beliefs have come to the surface on a few occasions, but that's such a small part of what the man is, it really is a non-issue with us any more.

"As he goes down this [national] trail they'll be digging up these things and saying, 'Oh, isn't it terrible he's a Christian.' They'll find out, as we did, that people like politicians who do stand for honesty and family. He doesn't allow his beliefs to stop him from representing the government and all of the people. He has the capacity to understand that people have different views and values. He respects that. He spends as much time talking with people in Lower Fairview, where most of the Native population lives, as he does in The Pines, where more middle-class people live. He's a very kind and generous man. I think the rest of Canada, if they get to know him, will come to see him the same way we do. They'll get past what his critics say about him and they'll see a good man there."

Being a Liberal in Red Deer is not really a ticket to higher office. The last time a Liberal won there was in a 1918 by-election. The voters came to their senses in the 1921 general election and booted him out. However, in Day's first election race in 1986, Liberal Don Campbell, principal of G.H. Dawe Community School, almost beat him, losing by just 389 votes.

Campbell, now retired, says he and Day have "always been on very good talking terms. Our philosophies are different. It doesn't mean his philosophy is right and I'm wrong, but he's a hard-working MLA. He does have very definite views. Often, politicians of all stripes come in under one guise or other and find it doesn't necessarily work with everybody, so they change their tune and come around more to the middle. They may get in by appealing to the extremists, but when they get there they find there is only so far that they can go, and they usually just conform. I don't think he has changed. I certainly have no regrets about him."

Day didn't have a job at the time, so he put food on the table with the $50 he made filling in for a local auctioneer on Tuesday nights. He also had some help from his family in the election campaign. His sister Rebecca moved into his house for six weeks. She and Day set up a door-knocking routine in which she would go to the door and say, "Hi, I'm Rebecca Reynolds. I'm campaigning for the Progressive Conservative candidate, Stockwell Day." At that point, she'd give him a hand signal and he'd come rushing up the walk.

"Then I'd feign surprise and say, 'Oh, here he comes now.' He was trying to look all athletic and splendid, although at the time he really wasn't all that athletic and splendid-looking, with those ridiculous, thick glasses he used to wear."

Rebecca says sometimes the reception was lukewarm. "He was perceived by some as a guy who had parachuted into the constituency and had no roots there. He was trying hard to play catch-up."

One vote they're sure he didn't get was that of a woman who came to the door one night. As Rebecca describes it, "While Stock was at the door going through his spiel, gesticulating, his arms waving madly, the woman had the door open just a bit. It was snowing, and the family cat decided this was a good time to escape. But because of the snow, Stock was stomping his feet up and down to keep warm, and he happened to stomp right on the cat's tail. But he was involved in his spiel — he didn't even notice. The cat did a series of big 180s and then began howling in despair, and the woman was very much put out.

"We left knowing we'd lost her vote, but then I looked down at Stock's shoes and I laughed so hard I collapsed in the snow. There were big chunks of cat fur sticking out either side of his one shoe."

Another vote they didn't get was on the occasion Rebecca accompanied her father, Stockwell Senior, on a door-knocking exercise. "Dad offered to do some campaigning and we put a lot of stock in family loyalty. I was elected to go with him. He would get perturbed when somebody would tell us that they weren't voting Conservative because they were Liberal or NDP, but he'd bite his tongue.

"But we went to this one door and the woman said, 'I'm not voting PC. Not only that, I don't like that candidate at all.' That was too much for Dad. He said, 'What the hell are you talking about?' I had to physically pull him off her stoop."

Her other memory of that campaign is the head-on picture of Day in his pamphlet that featured his thick glasses. "I pointed out that the picture made his head look skinny in the middle. It gave his head a fetching hourglass look. That was the last time he campaigned with glasses on." For her efforts, Rebecca was paid "with tons of fun and a pair of cowboy boots. I still have those boots."

Michael Dawe, Red Deer's official historian, was campaign manager for the local Liberals in 1986 and in two other campaigns against Day. He says that Day didn't emphasize his religious views as much during the 1986 campaign as he did in his failed nomination attempt in Lacombe three years earlier, where his campaign was "very much church-centred." Dawe notes that with each passing election, Day spends less time talking about that and more time on economic and law-and-order issues.

Dawe, who is also chairman of the Red Deer Regional Hospital Board, says that at one point on the election night of 1986, Day thought he had lost. "He actually finished second in the city of Red Deer, but the rural polls came in later and gave him his margin of victory. A lot of Conservative MLAs in this province have become lazy and complacent, but not Stockwell Day. He doesn't take anything for granted. He works hard.

"A lot of people like him, but as is the case with any charismatic, people who like him really like him, and people who don't, really don't.

You're rarely indifferent to the man. I would say he's enigmatic. The Stockwell Day you knew in Bentley is not the same Stockwell Day you knew in Red Deer. And the Stockwell Day in Red Deer is not the same Stockwell Day you knew in Kelowna. And the Stockwell Day in Montreal will be different again.

"He's very strong in his beliefs and he's a very good politician, but his views are not my views. He wouldn't be swayed by an opposing view on social issues or on fiscal issues. Is he a good listener? Well, that all depends on what you mean by listening. Certainly he'll listen. He's completely approachable. If you phone he'll return your call. He's very well organized. He'll sit down at the mall or at the farmer's market and have people talk to him about their concerns. He may listen to them, but I have never noticed any shift in his basic philosophy."

Long-time Red Deer Mayor Gail Surkan, once a Conservative director, says the community has an "excellent" working relationship with Day. "He's very frank and transparent as to what his views are. But I've never felt that he visited them on anybody else.

"There will always be for some people some concern when dealing with somebody who they feel may hold different views, regardless of what those views are," she says. "I respect that and Stock respects that. He has learned to work with it. He sets up a table down at the mall or at the farmer's market and he'll talk to anybody about whatever they want to talk about. People here know him not just as a skilful politician, but as an energetic and entertaining individual. He has an exceptional gift of humour. He does lots of impressions of famous people and is hotly sought after as a speaker. He's good at using his energy to stay connected to his community and he has been good at translating what he has said he is going to do into action. He doesn't confront people with his views and he knows it's not just a personal game — he has to espouse the views and policies of the party and the government — and he does that well. People see he is prepared to invest himself in getting work done for everybody. He doesn't spend all his time promoting his own personal values."

After winning the election, Day didn't waste any time trying to convince the people of Red Deer he was serious about his promises to keep in constant touch with the folks back home. Just three weeks later, he opened his first constituency office in room 403 of the Professional Building, right across from City Hall, promising it would be open from 9 A.M. to 1 P.M. weekdays, and pledging to spend a lot of time there himself when the legislature was not in session.

Day also set up an office in Edmonton and rented an apartment there, which he shared that first summer with his wife, Val, and three sons, Logan, then 13, Luke, 11, and Ben, 9. Day's workday started at 7 A.M. and usually went until 11 P.M. In July he was appointed to three select standing committees: the all-party Law and Regulations committee, the Private Bills committee, and the Legislative Offices committee. By the end of that month he was also named to a committee to evaluate all institutions receiving money from the provincial social services department. "It puts me in a position of learning a lot of the ropes in a hurry," he said. "You want to be conversant with everything that's going on. I don't know if there's any way to avoid first-year overload."

The first motion he made in the legislature came on July 9, when he proposed a committee to establish a system of incentives to reward government employees who come up with ideas to either save the government money or increase government efficiency, similar to incentive systems used in private companies. "It wouldn't be just a token reward," he said. "If we saved $50,000, the reward might be along the $5,000 range."

In November, Day and his Red Deer South colleague, John Oldring, were the only area MLAs who supported mandatory seat-belt use in Alberta. At the time, Alberta and Prince Edward Island were the only two provinces without such a law.

That same month, Day found himself embroiled in what would

become a regular feature of his career as a fiscal conservative. He had to fend off complaints from the Red Deer chapter of Pensioners Concerned, who were upset about a pending four-dollar-a-day increase for residents of nursing homes, auxiliary hospitals, and mental hospitals, denying the charge that the government was asking the sick and elderly to bear the brunt of provincial budget cuts. "The perspective seems to be that we are zeroing in on seniors and that is simply not the case. We are going to be seeing cuts across the board."

In February, sitting on a panel with two MLAs, a Liberal and an NDP, Day faced criticisms from his political opponents and from two hundred students at Red Deer College, who were upset over provincial grant reductions, tuition hikes, and changes to student loans. Day declared that even after the 3% cut in grants, Alberta was spending more on education than any other province. He professed to be "having a hard time trying to convince the man on the street that you [students] can't come up with another $45 a semester."

In April of 1987, Day was named chairman of the newly formed Alberta Tourism Educational Council, a public/private initiative to set up degree-granting programs to attract young people to tourism as a career choice. In September, after Don Getty's government increased personal income taxes by 6.9 percent, Day called for a cap on tax increases. Speaking at a local town hall meeting, Day said that even though Albertans had the lowest provincial tax rates in Canada, "We are taxed enough. As we approach this next budget year I will be opposing any tax increases."

Responding to local complaints about strip shows in local bars — in particular a 1,200-name petition gathered by Free Methodist minister Doug Russell — Day promised to see if the shows could be banned under the Alberta Liquor Control Act (they couldn't). "It wouldn't bother me at all to see them closed down," he said. "Strip shows involve the exploitation of women and men. This isn't a personal crusade; I'm responding to a request from my constituents."

In June of 1988, Day made news again by calling on Alberta social services to pay more attention to the problems of two-parent families in order to avoid broken marriages. He conceded that the government does a lot to help families after couples split up, such as daycare subsidies for single parents. "But it is a little like acute hospital care; you have got to move toward prevention." Day was responding to a major study of families in New York, Florida, and Missouri, which found that family structure, not poverty, was the greatest single factor in juvenile crime.

During the next month he waded into a local dispute between the residents and owner of the Northwood Estates trailer park. The residents were fed up with poor road conditions and unkempt vacant yards in the trailer court, but the owner said the problem started when "some jerk phoned 15 of his neighbours . . . to cause trouble." Both sides were threatening court action, but Day acted as conciliator. He said later that problems settled amicably have a better chance of working out in the long run.

In August he got to brag about the new $21-million, five-thousand-seat Agri-Trade Complex to be built with provincial lottery revenues in Red Deer's Westerner Park.

In stark contrast to his first nomination meeting, Day, then 38, was renominated without any opposition in January 1989. About a hundred supporters braved a blinding snowstorm and bitter cold to show their support for him. Day easily won re-election in March, winning all but four of the polls and defeating his nearest challenger, Bernie Fritze, by more than 1,300 votes. Overall, the Tories won 59 seats, the NDP, 16, and the Liberals, 8.

In 1986 Day had promised the people of Red Deer something that was unheard of locally at the time: that he'd go door knocking in between elections so they'd have a chance to discuss their concerns directly with him. He did that regularly. He also set up a booth at the farmer's market on Saturday mornings and dropped into the local mall for meet-the-people sessions. However, Day never works on Sundays, saving that day for church, family, and rest.

Locals still remember the night in November 1990 when the winter's first snowfall came and the -15° Celsius weather felt like 40° below with the wind chill. Day, who lived in Oriole Park on the northwest side of town, had advertised in the local newspaper that he was going door knocking that night. More than one person was shocked when they answered the door and saw him standing there.

His younger brother Matthew lived with him in the summer of 1989, in a Hyde Park apartment building at 116th and Jasper in downtown Edmonton. Matthew, a piano player in a jazz trio, was working at a hotel then as a "luggage transfer engineer" and getting musical gigs at night. Stockwell would often arrive home late from the legislature and the two brothers would head off to Earl's Tin Palace for wings and nachos.

"He's really a clean freak," says Matthew. "He doesn't like germs. Going into public washrooms, he would open the door with his foot. He's a foot flusher, too. He doesn't like to touch anything in a washroom.

"One time I got into a cleaning spree and, as a 19-year-old bachelor would do, I used a face cloth to clean the bathroom. I Pine-Sol'd the sink, the tub, and even the toilet — had it spotless — wrung out the face cloth, and put it back on the towel rack.

"Then I went out to a gig and when I got back Stock was in bed asleep. But I noticed that the face cloth was wet, so I shook him and told him I'd cleaned the entire bathroom with it, including the toilet. He was up and out of bed and in the bathroom for a good 15 minutes, scrubbing himself with as hot a water as he could. I told him later I was helping him get over his germophobia."

Matthew remembers learning something about forgiveness from his big brother at a very early age. Day had taken some kids from a youth group skiing at the Overlander Lodge in Jasper, which his parents owned at the time. He had a trick of throwing a snowball up in the air as high as he could, and when everybody was looking up, he'd toss the snowball he had hidden in his other hand at somebody.

"I was just 8 or 9, and he threw it at me and accidentally hit me in the face with it. I was crying and going crazy and the other kids were laughing. I lost it, but Stock came over to me in front of all those kids and said, 'I'm sorry, would you forgive me for that?' He wasn't saying, 'Don't be a baby,' or something like that; he was owning right up to a wrong. I've seen that in him all his life."

Matthew remembers going to his brother's house in Red Deer that year for Thanksgiving dinner. "Some guy from the Michener Centre didn't have a place to go, so Stock brought him home to join the family for Thanksgiving. He did that sort of thing a lot.

"He doesn't like to talk about some of those things, but one time he was out running across the North Saskatchewan River and he noticed a girl was going to jump, so he stopped and began talking with her. He told another jogger to go and get help and he stayed with that girl, talking to her all the time, for about half an hour until somebody came to help her."

On April 19, 1989, Premier Don Getty named Day chief government whip, a move into the inner sanctum of the Tory government. As whip, he got to co-chair cabinet and caucus meetings along with Getty. "It's an influential position and it's one of confidence and trust in terms of working with MLAs and the contact with the MLAs and for keeping things working smoothly in caucus," said Day.

He was on his way up the political ladder.

5

COURTING CONTROVERSY

I n June 1987, Day had again been railing about taxes, only this time he was ticked at Brian Mulroney's federal Tories for overspending and overtaxing Canadians.

Introducing a private member's bill, Day called for the opposition parties to join him in a united front against the federal Tory budget. "I am first of all a small 'c' conservative and that comes before being a party person. The budget galls my small 'c' conservative beliefs, so I have no hesitation making my displeasure known to them."

The next month, writing a column in the *Red Deer Advocate*, Day attacked Ottawa's controversial Goods and Services Tax (GST), saying it would take cash out of people's pockets and lead to loss of purchasing power and a subsequent demand for higher wages. That in turn, he wrote, leads to a lower cash flow in Canadian companies and more unemployment. Day opined that low-income families would benefit but middle- and high-income earners would pay from five hundred to a thousand dollars more per year. Later that year, Day and his Red Deer legislative colleague, John Oldring, packed the Red Deer Altaplex with 3,500 people in a protest against the proposed GST. Day said the turnout sent a strong message, not only to Ottawa but to all levels of government. "I take it very seriously. It sharpens my own resolve to look at our own spending provincially." He felt that all governments have areas where they can cut spending, but the other side of the equation shows up when the "axe begins to fall and programs are cut. People generally howl as much as when their taxes go up."

In August, Day voted against a 30% pay increase for the 83 members of Alberta's provincial assembly that gave MLAs $57,505 a year in salary and expenses, up from $44,322, but announced he was going to accept it anyway. "I am not running around looking for the badge of courage. I just said what I had to say and did what I had to do. This was a business item on an agenda which I voted against and I lost the vote. I will continue on in my job to accept decisions that I lose as well as the ones I win." Day said he didn't like the idea of MLAs setting their own salaries, and proposed an independent panel of people from all walks of life be established to review increases in salaries and expenses.

In another column about that time, responding to questions about how he spends his time as an MLA, Day said weeks of 80 to 100 hours are not rare when the legislature is sitting, and he averages 60 hours when it is not in session. "Saturday lunch and afternoon I try to spend with my sons. Depending on the season, it could be the beach, or tennis, racquetball, etc. They're starting to beat me now so I can't relax. Many Saturday evenings involve a local or out-of-town function. Sunday is our church and family day and I am so grateful that most of our constituents are very understanding when I respectfully decline government-related functions that day."

Day first waded into the controversial area of family values in February 1990, when he declared that he was "really honoured" that Getty had appointed him chairman of the Premier's Council in Support of Alberta Families (PCSAF). He said the council was "looking at a constructive advisory role," and that its goal was to strengthen families, not to create controversy.

But a month later, Day, striding in where politicians usually fear to tread, attacked sex education programs being taught in Red Deer schools, citing what he called growing concern from constituents over the "increasingly graphic and extensive nature of sex education programs presented to increasingly younger students." Day's other complaint was that the programs were being taught in a "morally neutral" way. While they were intended to be preventative, he felt that offering them without a moral framework could have the opposite effect. "The bottom line is there is a growing body of literature suggesting that as sex education becomes more comprehensive there is a corresponding increase in sexual activity."

Over the years, Day's critics have accused him of attempting to ban sex education in the schools. He certainly made it clear he didn't like the way sex was being taught, but, agree with him or not, he didn't call for a ban. "When I have a parent tell me that students in a classroom situation were told to unroll condoms, put them over their fingers, and see what they taste like, I say that's going too far," he said. He also complained that one training course for instructors featured a movie called *Five Women Masturbating*.

Day introduced a private member's bill on April 10, 1990, citing a 1986 study that found a direct relationship between the Planned Parenthood type of sex education and an increase in teen pregnancies. He called for a "values-based model: also giving students the facts but strongly promoting values and positive direction and self-esteem." Day said when that type of curriculum was pioneered in 1983 and 1984, the number of pregnancies at the school dropped from 178 to 20 by 1986–87.

Still, critics at the time accused him of wanting to ban sex education. In a letter to the *Advocate*, responding to what he called "editorial misrepresentations and deliberate bias," Day wrote: "I am not against sex. (Ask my wife.) I am not against sex education. (Ask my kids.) I am for parental choice of what type of sex education kids should be getting." He offered to send anybody who called a transcript of his presentation on the subject.

In February 1992, Day, on behalf of the PCSAF, unveiled the Family Policy Grid — eight principles upholding family values — which he said would be used to help evaluate the impact of existing or proposed legislation on families. The grid, the outcome of 20 public workshops during 1991, would be used to get legislators to think of the family instead of just individuals. Some existing programs, such as farm loans, would benefit a couple more if they divorced and applied separately. The grid promised to recognize and support families, help families fulfil their roles and responsibilities, respect and understand the diversity of family life and needs, strengthen families to decrease potential for family crisis, and recognize family ties.

He managed to upset some single parents by saying that their children are more likely than children of two-parent families to suffer from psychological, drug, and alcohol problems, to commit crimes, and to kill themselves. "It's very insulting the way he describes the way single parents are raising kids," said Lynn Bailey, a single mother whose 10-year-old son was an honour student. But Day said his remarks weren't at all meant as an attack on single parents. "We also know that there are lots of kids from two-parent homes who get involved with social problems, but kids who have gone through the trauma of divorce and been raised by single parents are statistically more susceptible to social problems, emotional problems, behavioural problems. And that can all lead, in some cases, to juvenile crime. It can also lead to drug and substance abuse. . . . That's the statistical reality."

Statistics compiled at the time by PCSAF and Statistics Canada did show that 82 percent of Albertans who marry stay married to the same person until one of them dies. The 10 percent who divorce are more than twice as likely to divorce again. Eighty-six percent of Alberta children were living in two-parent homes, nearly 70 percent of them with their natural mother and father. But among children living with a single parent, crime, suicide, and drug addiction rates were almost one-third higher.

It didn't matter. The *Edmonton Journal* labelled Day "an ostrich" and a threat to Alberta's families, and the *Calgary Herald* ran an editorial cartoon implying that Day thought battered wives should stay with abusive husbands. Day told *Alberta Report,* "The point never was that single or divorced parents are bad parents. The majority are not. Rather it is important for people contemplating such a major decision [as divorce] to have all the facts before them. To know about the increased risk to their children, so they would treat divorce more seriously and do all they could to save their marriages first."

Sarah Huemmert, who was executive director of the family council, says she has "tremendous admiration for him. Working for him was not always fun, since we are at different ends of the political spectrum, but he was always respectful of my views and everybody else's views. When I describe Stock, I start with the word integrity. He was one of the hardest workers I ever met — very, very dedicated. I've never met a person like him.

"A lot of people are very afraid of Christians, for a good reason. Christians are in the business of imposing their views on people. You don't find that kind of imposition of values from other religions," she says. "Yes, Stock has strong personal values and, more than anybody I've ever seen, he is living his values. But I never saw him proselytizing, ever. He was a good-hearted person who tried to live Christ-like values. I've never known anybody who lived his values, who let his light shine, and didn't judge. He'd just give everybody the benefit, he never needed to be above anybody, and he never pulled rank."

After Huemmert's husband, Kurt, died suddenly in 1993, Day conducted the funeral service. "He doesn't have that male thing about being afraid to talk about feelings and personal issues. Even though he takes a hard position, he's not hard-nosed," she remembers.

Huemmert tells the story of a Russian man who came into Day's Red Deer office looking for help. He said he was broke, so Day gave him some money and told him that when he got a job he could pay him back. "Of course, Stock never saw him again. But he just laughed about it; he didn't get angry. Because what matters to him is what he does, rather than what other people do. I've got a lot of friends who are afraid of him, and they tell me, 'You say one thing about him but we're reading another thing.' That's a real problem for Stock. But it wouldn't be if everybody knew him, believe me."

Day was thrilled in June 1990 when then Prime Minister Brian Mulroney appointed Alberta reformer Stan Waters to the Senate after Waters had won the first Alberta unofficial election to be a senator-in-waiting. "It's the beginning of the end of a truly useless Senate and the start of a truly effective Senate," Day enthused. "The move today is towards democracy around the world, whether it's Canada or the Berlin Wall. The walls are coming down and the wall to Senate reform will come down." Perhaps, but it hasn't yet.

One constituent who wasn't pleased with Day was Loretta Smith of Red Deer, who brought a 1,500-name petition to the legislature in December 1990 calling for more funding for public transportation. This came after city council had cut the evening bus schedule to four nights a week in favour of a dial-a-bus. But when Smith brought the matter to Day, she said, all he wanted to talk about was a dead pig — Francis, the freedom-loving pig, to be precise — that Day wanted invested into the Alberta Agricultural Hall of Fame. "I thought he was joking," Smith said. "He's my MLA and he was talking about some pig and nothing about my petition." Day said the bus schedule was a "municipal matter," adding that Alberta already provided one of the highest levels of financial support for public transit in Canada. Unhappy with Day, Smith gave her petition to an NDP member, who read it the next day in the legislature. Still fuming, she said, "I think their priorities are a little askew if they're more concerned about pigs than real-life problems."

In April of 1991, Day was one of 16 MLAs named to a special all-party committee on constitutional reform. The committee spent a good chunk of time touring the province and holding public hearings to discuss Alberta's role in Canada. In January 1992, however, Day raised eyebrows when he complained to a Commons-Senate unity panel in Edmonton that Ottawa should not require a certain percentage of federal civil servants to be bilingual. Day said the province provides services in French where the population warrants it, "but to require that a number — whatever the percentage — be fluent in both languages is what irritates people. My point is that it's a problem."

Liberal Senator Pierre de Bané, a former Trudeau cabinet minister, shouted, "Rubbish. I just can't sit by and hear this rubbish." He accused Day of spreading ignorance. According to the federal Treasury Board, of the 13,324 federal civil service jobs in Alberta at the time, 435, or 3.3 percent, were classified as bilingual. But Day said Alberta's figures showed that 27 percent of federal jobs in the province required bilingualism and were therefore out of reach for most people in the province. Gaetan Perron, vice-president of the Francophone Association of Central Alberta, told the *Advocate* that Day was "not helping the country." He said that 150,000 Albertans speak French, and that Day's comments, combined with Premier Don Getty's criticism of official bilingualism, "only fuel the fire" dividing French and English.

Day's comment that enforced bilingualism "irritates" people in Alberta is another one of those quotes that has been spun well beyond its original context. It is generally presented in a way that leaves the impression Day was opposed to French-language services and was demanding everybody in Alberta be served in English. Clearly, many Albertans *were* irritated by bilingual job classifications, as many Canadians in other provinces were, and are. "All I wanted was to discuss it," said Day after the meeting, adding that he understood why politicians are afraid to broach the subject after his experience of being misquoted and portrayed as an anti-French bigot by the Edmonton media.

Day was busy on other fronts during the spring of 1992, although none of them as controversial as his intervention on bilingualism. He introduced a motion to stop "double-dipping," so MLAs and former ministers couldn't collect their pensions until they retired entirely from government service. He proposed the Vulnerable Persons Act to protect caregivers and vulnerable clients who want to report abuse. He was named to head an all-party review of MLA salaries and benefits, and later recommended 5 to 10% pay cuts to set an example of fiscal restraint. He called for curbs on provincial politicians who take their spouses on government business trips at taxpayers' expense. And he was outraged over the conditional release of two prisoners who later killed an Edmonton police officer. "Our jails should not be perceived as happy havens offering college degrees, Saturday night lobster and muscle building programs," he said. "Part of prevention means effective deterrents, including tough productive work time and having judges who aren't afraid to send violent criminals away for a long time."

When Don Getty announced he was stepping down, Day supported his Red Deer South colleague, Family and Social Services Minister John Oldring, during the first round of the leadership race. But when it came down to Ralph Klein and Health Minister Nancy Betkowski (who, as Nancy MacBeth, is now Alberta's Liberal leader), Day says, "I resumed my position as party whip" and remained neutral.

It didn't hurt him. In December, Klein booted Oldring out of his cabinet and elevated Day to labour minister. Oldring, who admitted to being "a little disappointed," nonetheless praised the selection of Day. "I think he's one of the bright lights in cabinet and one of the most talented people there." As for Day, he said his goal would be "enhancing the worklife of Albertans," and his biggest challenge would be to maintain his close ties to local constituents. He said extra responsibilities "can shield some ministers from what's going on in the streets. But you can't let the portfolio drive our calendar." He didn't.

What he did do, however, was announce on his third day as a minister that he planned to use early retirement and attrition to trim the five-hundred-member staff of his department. "I believe my responsibility, number one, is to the taxpayers — and the taxpayers are looking for increased efficiency in terms of delivering government services," he said.

Local trade unionists had been applauding Day's performance as an MLA, but they were withholding their judgment on his selection as labour minister until they saw what he did. Connie Barnaby, a veteran of the Canadian Union of Public Employees (CUPE) and the losing NDP candidate against Oldring in Red Deer South, told the *Advocate* that Day had "represented the people in this area well. I certainly do not support the Tories or Klein's government, but I think Mr. Day is a good man." Day spoke at a Red Deer rally organized by CUPE to protest the government's proposal to bail out the ailing public pension fund. "He did give us the courtesy of appearing at our rally before and he seems to be listening well to his constituents. Whether he's going to listen to the workers as labour minister, I don't know."

Dianne Wyntjes, president of the six-thousand-member Red Deer and District Labour Council, said she was encouraged by Day's promise to make "enhancing the worklife of Albertans" his greatest goal. She felt that if he held to that ideal and worked on a consensus basis, then she expected Day to be open to the concerns of organized labour.

Things change. In an interview this year, Wyntjes, now a national representative for CUPE, told me, "contrary to popular opinion, he doesn't listen to other points of view. He's quite good in some ways when you meet him. You get the feeling you're the most important person in the world in that half hour. But in the end, it's what you can do with the issues that count, and we were completely discredited."

Wyntjes says she was speaking one year at the annual April 28 Day of Mourning, in recognition of workers killed or injured on the job, talking about the need for better workplace safety rules. "He came up to me afterwards and said my remarks were totally inappropriate and I should be ashamed of myself. I was shocked. I found it appalling for somebody who should recognize the value of people to say what he did. I wasn't impressed with him as a politician that day. I wish the man well, but to me the substance of a politician is how he deals with the various competing interests in society. In his case, I don't see much concern for any other interests but his own."

Day remembers the incident too, but not the way Wyntjes does. "Yes, I went up to her afterwards and I told her I was disappointed that her message was all death, ruin, and destruction, and the capitalist machine was killing people. I just pointed out that we'd made some real progress, that you could see the drop in workplace injuries and deaths. She was saying there had been no progress being made on behalf of workers — that was my complaint. Yes, there were still problems, but I thought it only fair to say there had been progress as well. But that was a very solemn forum. There were lots of people there, and there's no way that I would upbraid her like that in front of all those people." Alberta's death and work-injury rate fell from five workers per hundred in 1990 to 3.9 in 1992.

When Day took over the ministry, the Workmen's Compensation Board had a $600-million unfunded liability. In less than two years, he turned that around into a surplus while raising benefits to injured workers and lowering premiums. He cut his department's budget by 40 percent and, as part of implementing Ralph Klein's stringent fiscal restraint package, Day also used his consensus skills. Without breaking the collective agreement — as NDP Premier Bob Rae did in Ontario when he imposed a settlement on the unionized workers — Day persuaded the public service unions that it was in their interest and the interest of the province in general for them to take a 5% cut.

In January 1993, Day got himself into another public pickle when various arts groups went ballistic over newspaper reports that he wanted to stop all public funding for the arts. Once again, Day was attacked for something he hadn't said. What he did say was that in a time of restraint, he wanted to hear from Albertans what their ideas were for cutting government funding. He said cutbacks could include the arts, culture, MLA pensions, or big business, but he never said public funding of the arts should be nuked. "We have to look at everything we spend," Day said, "and everything people have to pay taxes on and see what changes can be made." No matter — reacting to Day and similar comments from two other ministers, two dozen representatives of Calgary's music, dance, theatre, visual arts, and cultural heritage communities held a special meeting to present a united front against what they called the government's "continuing attacks on arts funding." In an *Edmonton Journal* column, freelance writer Brad Welk wrote that Day's comments "degrade, demean and seriously damage the efforts of thousands of Alberta parents, teachers, and citizens who individually volunteer hundreds of hours to cultural activities."

But politics being what it is, a few days later Day was being publicly praised for ending months of government delay and appointing a 13-member committee to draft regulations to make midwifery legal in Alberta. Sheila Andersen, a Red Deer member of the Alberta Midwifery Task Force who was appointed to the committee, said it was "the last hurdle" before midwives could become certified in the province. She thanked Day for making it possible. "It's to his credit that he got things flowing so quickly," she said. Day said that midwifery "meets the needs of women, mothers and families in this province."

In June 1993, Day won an overwhelming majority in the provincial election, collecting 5,441 votes, almost twice as many as his nearest rival, Liberal Tony Connelly. "I'm overwhelmed with the show of support," he said. "I'm at a loss for words . . . I think it's a combination show of support for myself and Ralph [Klein] for sure."

Shortly after the campaign, Day, supporting the new welfare policy that put more onus on employable people to look for work or take training, said healthy, single people should be out working instead of collecting welfare. "They need more incentive to work. I know some people think we are being mean. But it is not mean to put more positive pressure on people to take more responsibility for themselves. There are jobs posted in the *Advocate* as we speak."

Patricia Wynne, coordinator of the Red Deer Food Bank, said more and more social workers were referring clients to the food bank. Day said churches and community agencies have always helped out people in need and they should continue that work.

Wynne, who ran the local food bank from 1990 to 1998, is the kind of person you'd expect to be critical of a fiscal hawk like Day. But she's not. "You won't get me to say anything bad about Stock Day," she told me in a telephone interview. "We were on opposite sides of the fence but we had a lot in common. We both believed in the same thing; we just had a different approach. We were able to keep a good professional relationship because we had a healthy respect for discussing issues and not personalities.

"He did listen. But he took the information and did whatever he felt was appropriate with it. That wasn't always what I felt was appropriate, but at least you know that he had listened to what you had said. To be able to work on opposite sides and still be able to come out with smiles and handshakes is a fine and rare thing.

"He struck me as a person who is truly interested in serving the people. He has the unique ability that my grandmother had too. Mom had ten kids. I was the last of her grandchildren. I was adopted. Yet whenever I was in her presence, she made me feel I was the only person in the world. Stockwell has that ability to go one-on-one with people and make them feel they're important and that he's personally interested in what they have to say. He's a very personable, caring, and ethical man. What he says comes from the heart, and that often gets politicians in trouble."

In July, Klein moved Day into his powerful inner cabinet. Day kept his labour job, became deputy house leader, and was named to the influential Agenda and Priorities committee and the six-member provincial Treasury Board. He said his top priority was to ensure the government stuck to its plan to wipe out Alberta's $3.2-billion deficit by 1997. It didn't.

In September, Day was one of seven Tories who broke with their own party to vote in favour of a Liberal-sponsored bill. The bill, which would have allowed voters to recall MLAs if there was 40% support in the riding to do so, was defeated after second reading.

In October, Alberta Justice Minister Ken Rostad said Ottawa should consider licensing prostitutes or establishing official brothels if it was serious about controlling the illegal sex trade. Day said that would just lead to more problems with prostitutes, pornography, and drugs. "We're never going to eliminate prostitution just like we're never going to eliminate drunk driving," said Day. "But if you remove the legal constraints, there will be an increase in the negative effects." He stated that Thailand and Amsterdam, where prostitution is legal, were facing serious problems with child pornography, child prostitution, illicit drugs, and a slave trade. "I have to look at that history and represent my constituents." He said he was sure they didn't support liberalization. A month later, Klein named Day as government house leader in addition to his other duties.

In June 1994, several Alberta businesses were pressuring Day to bring in right-to-work legislation to get rid of legislation that protected closed shops. Just 26 percent of Alberta's labour force was unionized and 70 percent of that total were public servants. Under a right-to-work law, non-union workers would be allowed to work on the same job site and in the same jobs as union workers. Veteran journalist Ted Byfield, the founder of *Alberta Report* and an Alberta institution in his own right, says he was at a businessmen's luncheon at that time where Day was the guest speaker. "They were really pressuring him to go for it and he had to deliver a message they didn't want to hear. But the way he did it was masterful. He told them that while he thought their arguments had merit, Alberta was just getting out of a recession, so do we really need to pick a fight with the labour unions over something as academic as this? He persuaded them of this. He stood his ground. It's easy to tell people what they want to hear. It's not so easy to tell them what they don't want to hear and [have them] still go away thinking you're a good guy."

Another frequently reported criticism of Day's social conservatism is that in 1994 he wanted John Steinbeck's novel *Of Mice and Men* removed from the schools because of its profane language. Day was attacked by critics as a book burner. The thing is, it wasn't Day who wanted the book banned, it was the Red Deer South MLA, Victor Doerksen. Day said at the time that children "don't need to be exposed to the name of Jesus Christ being taken in a blasphemous sense," but he did not advocate banning the book. He did say Doerksen had the right to present that view on behalf of his constituents.

A couple of weeks later, however, Day was ticked off by some of the language cropping up in the legislature. Day was upset with an expletive he says Liberal MLA Danny Dalla-Longa shouted during a debate, and asked Speaker Stan Schumacher to get tough with MLAs who misbehaved. What did Dalla-Longa say? Day said that he shouted "the street term which refers to fecal matter coming from the male gender of the bovine species," that there were children in the public gallery, and that "taxpayers are not impressed by the antics that go on."

In November, Red Deer's Christmas Bureau, a charity that had provided toys for 1,996 children the previous Christmas, announced it was setting up shop downtown, rent-free except for utilities, in the former Alberta Liquor Control Board building. The charity credited Day for securing the spot. "He went to bat for us," said president Mickey McMaster. "That's the best location we've had for a long time."

In February 1995, Day announced that six hundred provincial employees would be out of work by March 31, bringing the total cuts to about seven thousand since the Klein government took office two years earlier. "We're reducing our government and the cost of government so that we have a recession-proof operation," he said. "No matter if oil prices are up or down, we're going to be running government without having to borrow money and go further in debt." He said people were being treated "fairly and with dignity, realizing that it is never an easy time to face losing a job." Day said the government would do all it could to cushion the blow through severance packages and counselling.

Day, like fellow Alliance leadership contenders Preston Manning and Tom Long, makes no secret of the fact that he is anti-abortion. In April 1995 he joined 16 other Alberta cabinet ministers and backbenchers in agreeing with a pro-life activist group, the Committee to End Tax-Funded Abortions, that was calling for an end to tax-funded abortions except in cases where the mother's life was at risk. They weren't trying to ban abortions, but they were arguing that the taxpayers shouldn't pay for them. While Ralph Klein said he'd rather stay clear of the issue, Day and the others said their mail and phone calls were overwhelmingly in favour of de-insuring abortion. "We need to analyze the legal and medical aspects of it . . . also the moral implications," said Day. He felt that if physicians determined that a deformed fetus made abortion medically necessary, for example, many disabled constituents would be alarmed. "There are a lot of couples willing to adopt any baby."

Critics immediately attacked Day for wanting to cut funding even to victims of rape and incest, and to this day journalists — and Day's political opponents — continue to repeat this charge against him. In her June 14, 1995, *Calgary Herald* column, for example, Susan Ruttan wrote, "presumably he [Day] thinks raped women should do their civic duty and bear the unwanted child." Again Day denied saying it, and nobody in the media had actually quoted him — or produced a quote later on — using the words *rape* and *incest*. Reporters had inferred it because Day had said many couples were eager to adopt, "be it a product of any situation." In fact, it was Day's Red Deer South colleague, Victor Doerksen, who had mentioned rape and incest. But even there, Doerksen had explained to a reporter from his local newspaper that abortion funding by Alberta Health wouldn't be necessary in cases of victims of rape and incest, because the Alberta Crimes Compensation Board would cover it. He said that it was "a moot point" from a financial viewpoint because "in those cases, compensation is already available." That detail was ignored in the ensuing outcry by pro-choice advocates and their media supporters.

Day, of course, was once again painted as holding an extreme position on the issue. He claimed to be in the mainstream, and he was. An Angus Reid poll on the question of tax-funded abortions had found that just 30 percent of Prairie province respondents felt the government should pay for all abortions. Sixty-four percent were either against any medicare coverage of abortions or approved of it only in special circumstances, such as when the mother's life was at risk, which is where Day stood on the issue.

———

Fast forward to March 30, 2000, during Day's opening leadership-campaign foray into Ontario. The *Ottawa Citizen* headline declared: "Day Defends 'Mainstream' Views." The issues, of course, were abortion and capital punishment. Day was quoted as saying that Canadians were split 50-50 on abortion. "I'm in the mainstream." But Cindy Recker, director of the Canadian Abortion Rights Action League's education program, cited a 1998 Environics poll showing that 78 percent of respondents agreed that the decision should be left up to the woman and her doctor. "He is not a mainstream politician [on that issue]," she said.

But is that true? Even most pro-life people would agree that if there is to be an abortion, it should be performed by a doctor, and therefore the decision is between the woman and the doctor. But that is not the same as saying that 78 percent believe that abortion on demand is acceptable, although the way the poll is used by abortion activists implies that.

University of Lethbridge sociology professor Reginald Bibby, author of the best-selling book *The Bibby Report*, devotes much of his time to tracking Canadian attitudes on issues ranging from their favourite sports and talk-show hosts to religion, political leadership, the environment, crime and punishment, national unity, and, of course, the social issues of abortion, homosexuality, and capital punishment.

In his 1995 survey, Bibby found that 95 percent of Canadians — and that includes Day — agree that a woman should have access to a legal abortion when her health is seriously endangered, and 89 percent favour access to abortion in the case of rape. Beyond that, however, Canadian attitudes are a little less cut and dried. Those who oppose abortion of any kind represent only 10 percent of the population, but, Bibby writes, "the other 90 per cent are far from pro-choice. When the health of the mother or the unborn child is not involved, many Canadians have significant reservations." How significant? Well, Bibby found that 39 percent of Canadians favoured abortion "on demand," that is, unrestricted access to the procedure, a tiny increase of two percentage points from ten years earlier. But support for abortion drops to 54 percent in cases where the reason for the abortion is strictly economic, for example, the family has a low income and can't afford more children. It drops to 48 percent if the reason for the abortion is the woman is not married and does not want to marry the father, and to 46 percent if she is married and does not want to have any more children. What's more, all of these numbers have stayed pretty consistent since Bibby first began tracking them in 1975.

Bibby sums up that if strict pro-lifers are a 10% minority and pro-choicers are close to 40%, "we are left with the conclusion that the majority of Canadians — some 50 percent — take neither of these two absolutist positions. They are highly situational." So when Day says his position is mainstream, he has a point. Given the actual numbers — as opposed to the overwhelming media bias — his position hardly qualifies as extreme.

On September 26, 1995, Day got out of his car just before the 9 P.M. closing time to run into the downtown Co-op store in Red Deer. Day didn't know it at the time, but a man had just brandished what looked like a handgun (it turned out to be a pellet pistol) in the store's pharmacy and demanded prescription drugs. Just as Day entered the store, the man, wearing a balaclava, rushed at full speed out the door, almost bumping into Day. Realizing it was a robbery, Day, who was wearing a shirt, slacks, and dress shoes, took off after him. After several blocks the man paused and threw off some clothes. "I shouted to him to stop, and he told me to do something else," recalls Day. Then the chase resumed, back and forth through various back alleys, until the man emerged about four blocks from the Co-op. He dashed across the road into an apartment building and was buzzed in. Day arrived just as the door was closing. "So I just put both my hands on all the intercom buttons at once and buzzed everybody and figured somebody would hit it." Somebody did, and Day chased the fugitive up four flights of stairs before he disappeared into an apartment. Then Day banged on various apartment doors until one was opened; he asked the woman inside to call the police. It took two RCMP officers just four or five minutes to arrive on the scene. In the meantime, Day had been clomping around the hallway outside the suspect's apartment, hoping to sound like a crowd in order to deter the suspect from bolting.

The police quickly persuaded the two men in the apartment to come out. "I was pumped," says Day, adding that he never intended to get into a fight with the suspect, but felt it was a person's civic duty to help police. It would have been different if he'd known about the gun. "I suppose we all like to think we're brave, but if I'd seen a guy waving a gun I might have let my shoes slow me down a little."

Ten days later, Glen David Siford, 27, of Red Deer, pleaded guilty to two counts of robbery and wearing a disguise while committing an offence. Provincial Court Judge Dave MacNaughton sentenced the former heroin addict to three years in jail. Two months later, Day's eldest son, Logan, then 23 and a security officer at Safeway, tackled a shoplifter after a 15-minute foot chase through yards and alleys. In May 1997, the elder Day was one of five people honoured by the Red Deer Optimist Club for "holding respect for the law."

In May 1989, without first discussing it with the Tory caucus, then Labour Minister Elaine McCoy announced a plan to extend human rights protection to homosexuals. Most of that caucus, Day included, were strongly opposed. Day, who was party whip at the time, accused McCoy of having "pre-empted the caucus process. . . . Most people agree that we need to have protective legislation for reasons of religion, ethnic origin and gender," he said. "But they feel no group should have special protective legislation based on sexual activity whether it is a group of heterosexuals or homosexuals or sexual abstainers."

In the spring of 1994, Justice Anne Russell of the Court of Queen's Bench in Edmonton ruled that Alberta's human rights law contravened the Constitution by failing to protect homosexuals from discrimination, in what immediately became known as the Vriend case. The ruling set off a firestorm of debate in Alberta, which hasn't been resolved yet. The issue involved not only the question of homosexual rights, but the whole area of judicial activism. Many Canadians are uneasy with judge-made law that often goes against the express wishes of the politicians who wrote the Charter of Rights and Freedoms and against prevailing public attitudes.

The media spin is that Vriend was fired from his job as a teacher at King's University College in Edmonton, a fundamentalist Christian school, because he was homosexual. While that version of the story makes a complicated reality easier to understand — and provides better ammunition to use against critics of the court ruling — it's not entirely accurate. Yes, Vriend was homosexual. And yes, he was fired by the college in 1991, but only after he began to get involved in in-your-face homosexual activism, such as wearing T-shirts to school proclaiming "I'm gay and proud of it," and after he began cohabiting with another man. But what is lost in the debate is that Vriend would have been fired had he been cohabiting with a woman who was not his wife, or for contravening any number of moral strictures to which the school adhered. The officials of this Christian school believed they had the right to demand their teachers adhere to Christian values.

Vriend didn't agree. He complained to the Alberta Human Rights Commission, but it refused to hear his complaint because sexual orientation was not a designated ground for discrimination. So Vriend then sued the government, and in 1994 the Edmonton court ruled that sexual orientation should be read into the human rights legislation. That decision was overturned by the Alberta Court of Appeal. Finally, in 1998, the Supreme Court of Canada upheld the original Vriend ruling, ordering Alberta to amend its human rights legislation.

Day argued all along that the legislature, not the courts, should decide such issues. He made it clear where he stood. Day stated that religious institutions "are supposed to have protection" for their theological beliefs, adding that "nobody gets fired because they're a homosexual. They get fired if they don't do their job." He said there were likely several homosexuals working in his department, but "as long as that's not interfering with their work, that's no reason to fire them." In Vriend's case, said Day, he contradicted the employer's religion by openly advocating homosexuality. Another problem, he felt, is that there is no adequate definition for what constitutes sexual orientation. "What about the next step: those who lobby for sex with children? These are very large and active national interests."

The court case was never about Vriend's being fired for being a homosexual. It was about whether sexual orientation should be read into Alberta's human rights legislation. The court ruled that Vriend had the right to have his complaint against the Christian school heard by the human rights tribunal.

Shortly before that 1998 Supreme Court ruling, Ralph Klein named Day to a four-member cabinet committee to look at legal options, should the province lose its case. Critics attacked Klein for putting Day and Justice Minister Jon Havelock on the committee. Then the NDP leader, Pam Barrett, complained, "They're stacking the deck against human rights," no doubt preferring to have the deck stacked on her side instead. Day said that if the court ruled against Alberta, the provincial government might use the notwithstanding clause of the Charter of Rights and Freedoms, but not without first consulting the public across the province. In the end, Klein declined to use the notwithstanding clause to override the Supreme Court decision. Day, admitting his disappointment, said, "The song says you don't always get what you want." He said the four-member committee would "build fences" around some of the more contentious issues, such as same-sex marriages and adoptions by homosexuals.

While all this was going on, Day got into political hot water again. In August 1997 he complained about a $10,000 grant to the Red Deer museum to pay for photographs, taped conversations, and historical documents of the life experiences of local homosexuals and their organizations and events. Day said the museum isn't the proper place to advance the "cause" of homosexuals, and certainly not at public expense. He said people don't want to visit the museum to be "confronted" by someone's sexual choice. Day asked Community Development Minister Shirley McClellan to cancel the grant, but was told it was too late because the money had already been sent out. Museum director Wendy Martindale responded that the homosexual community was under-represented in traditional historical research. "We knew it was a project like this that had a potential to get a reaction like this. I'm disappointed this has happened but it reinforces to me that the experience one has as a gay or lesbian is different. It reinforces the need to do this work." Asked about the controversy later, Ralph Klein said Day was only doing his job representing the views of his constituents.

In September 1999, *Calgary Herald* columnist Don Martin obtained a copy of the museum's 34-page study. Martin, no fan of what he calls Day's "ideological tailoring," says that the study does not promote homosexual lifestyles as Day had feared. But, he said, "What the researchers concluded, for our $10,000 investment, is severely questionable and at times almost laughable." The study was based on a tiny sample of 19 participants, with three entire interviews lost because of a tape-recorder malfunction. In it the interviewees lament its being socially acceptable for women to call each other "honey" in public, "whereas with men it would be a shocker." Martin, a social liberal, writes, "Okaaaay, call me old-fashioned but I'd look twice at men yelling 'hi honey' to each other across the parking lot, too." Martin said the study disdains the "automatic assumption of opposite-sex partnerships" when people at the door "dare to ask a gay male if his wife is home. Well, sorrrrry, but what are they to do? Ask every male who answers the door if his gay lover is home?"

In an April 3, 1999, interview of Day by Linda Frum of the *National Post*, Frum cites the *Toronto Star*'s neat summation of Day "by calling him a 'gay-bashing abortion-hater' who will not be able to sell his ideas in Ontario and the Maritimes." Day calls that an "unfair characterization. I do not think laws should change to accommodate homosexual marriage.

But how do you justify the leap from that to calling someone a gay-basher? Obviously people should not be discriminated against for their sexual choices when it comes to such issues as employment or housing. But to go from that to request that a very significant public policy change to accommodate what they are doing, I say, 'wait a minute.'"

On the question of the museum grant, Day told Frum, "That was a constituency issue. The museum in Red Deer received a very specific grant from the provincial government to be used in the museum. And that museum has a lot of needs. I thought the application of $10,000 of public money to pursue the issue of homosexual history did not make sense at all."

So just how extreme *is* Day when it comes to homosexual issues? To hear the media and homosexual activists tell it, he's extreme even by extremist standards. But is he really? In *The Bibby Report,* Lethbridge sociologist Reginald Bibby tracks Canadian attitudes towards homosexuality from 1975 to 1995. He has discovered that, while attitudes are shifting, just 32 percent of Canadians in 1995 (up markedly from 14 percent 20 years earlier) believe that homosexuality is "not wrong at all." Another 16 percent say it is "sometimes wrong," 7 percent say it is "almost always wrong," and 45 percent say it is "always wrong."

Bibby writes, "Significantly, between 1990 and 1995, during a time of considerable debate about same-sex rights, support for the idea of gays and lesbians receiving 'the same rights as other Canadians' dropped from the 1990 high of 80 percent to 67 percent." This is perhaps why federal Liberal Justice Minister Anne McLellan amended her same-sex benefits legislation to define marriage as "the lawful union of one man and one woman to the exclusion of all others." That specifically excludes homosexual "marriages," but the media has not gone after McLellan for her gay-bashing, intolerant homophobia. Why not?

Day took over as social services minister in June 1996, promising no radical changes from his predecessor's plans to reduce welfare rolls and give communities more responsibility for running social services programs. Some expressed concern at the time that Day's appointment would bring a harder edge to the government's welfare policies. However, Rod Adachi, president of the Alberta Association of Social Workers, told the *Calgary Herald* two months after Day's appointment, "He seems quite open to us. He seems to be a man of principle. He seems to have his own set of values and is guided by them."

One of Day's first moves was to bump people on medical assistance up to disability classification, giving them higher benefits. Liberal social services critic Alice Hanson said, "I haven't got a thing to complain about." Now that he had the power, Day brought in the Protection of Persons in Care Act, which he'd first introduced as a private member's bill five years earlier. The act's aim is to protect both staff and clients in hospitals, lodges, group homes, and nursing homes from physical, sexual, financial, or psychological abuse.

In January 1997, Day said he was hearing from an increasing number about "people's lives being wrecked by their addictions" to video lottery terminals (VLTs). He thought that moving the machines from hotels and bars to designated casinos might ease the problem. In July, Day criticized his own government's new casino rules that allowed casinos to extend their hours, open on Sundays, double their slot machines, and serve liquor at gaming tables.

Day won another landslide victory in March 1997, capturing 55.5 percent of the popular vote, easily defeating Liberal Norm McDougall and two other candidates.

It didn't take him long to create another controversy, this time by saying something he would have been better off to have kept to himself. Speaking at the right-wing Roots of Change conference in Calgary, Day remarked that convicted child-killer Clifford Olson should be released into the general prison population so the "moral prisoners" could deal with him. He was attacking the federal Liberals' refusal to rescind the so-called "faint-hope" clause, which gives convicted murderers who are sentenced to life in prison the opportunity to seek parole after 15 years. "People like myself say, 'Fix the problem. Put him in the general [prison] population. The moral prisoners will deal with it in a way which we don't have the nerve to do.'"

Attempting to wiggle his way out of his problem, Day said later that he wouldn't speculate on what would happen to Olson in the general prison population because he didn't want to "fall into the trap of encouraging people to break the law. My suggestion is that in some ways prisoners have a higher morality in terms of justice than the Liberals do. They would have less fear of letting their sense of justice be known." In a subsequent open letter, Day claimed he was a victim of a media assault. "Conferences which encourage free-wheeling discussions on social ills can be energetic, provocative and thought-provoking," he wrote. "However, the unfortunate price of free speech these days can be the risk of a media assault on one sentence lifted from its broader context." It happens to Day more than most.

Day's worst verbal gaffe came in April 1999, when he attacked a Red Deer lawyer and school trustee, Lorne Goddard, for defending convicted pedophile Kevin Valley's right to possess child pornography. (Valley ultimately got six years in prison.) During the trial Goddard tried unsuccessfully to apply the controversial B.C. ruling that struck down child-porn possession laws as unconstitutional — a decision currently before the Supreme Court. The issue prompted Day to write to the *Advocate* that, while he took no issue with Goddard's right to defend his client, the lawyer's reported statement "went far beyond that. He is reported to have said that he actually believes the pedophile had the right to possess child porn."

In May, Justice Minister Jon Havelock ordered legislative members to stop commenting publicly about cases before the courts. "It is very important that we ensure that the process is seen to be fair, that it is not undermined," said Havelock. The next day, Ralph Klein scolded Day for his actions. "I talked to Stock about it," said Klein. "I agree that it's inappropriate to discuss matters that are before the courts. But he did say to me that he was concerned that this individual's personal views went beyond his duties as a lawyer and he was more concerned because this individual is a member of the Red Deer school board."

In June Goddard filed suit against Day, seeking $300,000 in general damages and $300,000 in punitive damages. "As a result of the malicious publication of the false and defamatory statements, [Goddard's] reputation has been personally adversely affected in the course of his professional activities as a lawyer and school board trustee," the court papers read.

Day replied that he still believed Goddard needed to "clarify" his personal views on possession of child pornography. "He feels he has been unfairly treated. But certainly my own comments have always been that he has been a fine and upstanding member of our community and he needs to clarify his views before the next school board election, because he is an elected official as well as being a lawyer." In late August, however, Day sent Goddard a letter of apology, which was published in several Alberta newspapers. The letter stated, "The arguments I made . . . were not intended to address your own personal beliefs on the question [of child pornography]." Goddard said, "The letter will help, but I still have to deal with the consequences," and that he would continue his suit despite the apology.

In his statement of defence, filed September 2, Day claims he had a legal, social, and moral duty to say what he did. He said his statements "amount to political comment on an issue of public importance, namely child pornography, and such comments are accordingly protected either by the defence of qualified privilege or bona fide fair comment on matters of public interest."

The controversy took a new twist that same month, when it was learned that Alberta taxpayers would pick up the tab for Day's defence, through the government's risk management fund. Day stated that the lawsuit "arose as a result of my duties as an MLA. The government, just as does any corporate entity, insures its employees." But Alberta Liberals asked ethics commissioner Robert Clark to investigate whether Day was violating the Conflict of Interest Act by having his fees covered by the fund. Day then asked the justice department to make all the decisions concerning funding of his legal expenses.

At one point Day had planned to raise funds privately, through a citizens' legal defence fund, to pay the bills, but Clark said that would be a breach of the Conflict of Interest Act. The ethics commissioner ruled that Day had done nothing wrong in the decision by the risk management fund to cover his legal costs. Day said, "I'll have to abide by the ruling. MLAs should not have to run around fundraising from private sources to perform government business."

The ruling affected NDP Leader Pam Barrett, who had earlier been critical of Day, remarking, "I don't see any reason he should not be paying his own legal bills." But Barrett and her party were being sued by the Calgary-based Health Resources Group for comments she made about its plans to offer private, for-profit hospital care. She too had wanted to set up a fund to pay the legal bills.

In late November 1999, Day launched a personal Internet Web site to defend himself against Goddard's charges, citing his need to cope with an overwhelming volume of calls about the case. In December, Day claimed that Goddard was making "vexatious" and "improper" allegations against him. Goddard had originally been seeking $600,000, but decided to seek unspecified "aggravated damages" after Day set up his Web site.

The following February, a legislature committee approved new guidelines for lawmakers who want to use taxpayer-funded insurance when they are sued. The guidelines provide politicians with more information about their coverage and set out a new process for applying for funds. On February 17, court documents indicated that Day's defamation trial will begin on November 6 and last for ten days. And on April 19, Justice Patrick Sullivan of the Court of Queen's Bench ruled that Day will not have to turn over documents from cabinet meetings in the case.

And the beat goes on.

6

—

PAYING THE PIPER

—

When most people think of Puerto Rico, they think of splashing in the Caribbean Sea, sunning on pristine beaches, shopping in San Juan, or playing golf on seaside links. When Stockwell Day thinks of Puerto Rico, he thinks of tax cuts. In every speech he delivers, Day loves to tell his audience that the small, self-governing Commonwealth of the U.S., with 3.5 million people, cut personal income taxes by 30 percent in 1987. What happened next? Well, the following year the number of Puerto Ricans filing income tax returns increased by an astounding 50 percent. "Reducing taxes," he says, "makes people happy."

That should be a self-evident truth. All those in favour of higher taxes please raise your hands. But the real question is not whether you want lower taxes — of course you do — but can governments deliver them and still meet the ever-increasing fiscal demands of society? Day says yes. And as one of the leading Canadian advocates — and practitioners — of tax slashing, the evidence seems to support his rhetoric.

Day uses his hands-on experience in dealing with fiscal realities as one of his strongest arguments against Preston Manning's lack of experience in government and the backroom origins of Alliance leadership candidate Tom Long. "I've actually had to get out there and do it," he says. "The fact is that I've been able to take policy and make it work on the street. Every year I was treasurer, taxes went down. We had a surplus. I brought in legislation that pays down debt in an obligatory way."

There's no doubt many Canadians are ticked about their taxes. Even federal Finance Minister Paul Martin's February 29, 2000, budget offered $39.7 billion in income tax cuts over the next five years, although all but $16 billion is not scheduled until years four and five of his five-year plan. Still, Martin pleasantly surprised most observers by killing the dreaded "bracket creep" when he indexed income tax rates to inflation. Day, who had characterized the bracket-creep windfall gains as "legalized theft," beat Martin to the punch when he killed them in his last Alberta budget, just five days earlier.

While Martin's cuts were generally welcomed after years of relentless tax hikes, most of the reductions are what the *National Post* described as "merely contingent promises that are not even scheduled to begin until 2004–2005. These are less tax cuts than election promises." A *National Post*/COMPAS Inc. poll in April 1999 found that 85 percent of respondents were "upset" by the taxes they paid relative to the perceived value of government services received. A *Reader's Digest*/Gallup poll published in June 1999 found that 83 percent of respondents felt their total tax bills were "too high."

As of 1999, the average Canadian was paying 46 cents in taxation for each loonie earned. Increasing taxes meant that real incomes (adjusted for inflation) actually dropped about 8 percent during the 1990s, compared to an increase of 10 percent during the same period in the United States. In this country's major trading partner and competitor, the average tax bill is about 25 percent less than ours. And it's not because we have medicare and they don't. Whether you measure government health spending as a percentage of GDP or on a per capita basis, Americans spend more on health care than Canadians.

Even when you add the enormous military spending of the U.S., compared to the pittance we dole out to our dispirited Armed Forces, American governments still extract 10 percent less from their total economy than what Canadians pay to their governments. For those of you who feel you've been working harder but have less to show for it, chances are that you do. During the past ten years in the U.S., real, after-tax income increased 18 percent. In Canada, it dropped 2 percent.

"If you feel like the wheels are spinning," says Day, "in fact they are." As one of the few politicians in Canada who has been not only demanding lower taxes for years, but actually implementing them, Day appeared on April 13, 2000, on the CBC Radio phone-in program "Ontario Today." He was asked by host Dave Stephens if he "sees taxes as a punishment."

"Most people do," said Day. "Most people see taxes . . . first of all as necessary. Taxes are necessary . . . but increasingly Canadians are seeing the present level of tax as punitive . . . when you take in all our taxes at all levels . . . [and] in some cases 50 percent of your hard-earned money gets taken from you. Then when people look at how it's presently being spent, when the federal Liberal government says they're having difficulty accounting for a billion dollars in one department alone, HRDC [which Day says stands for 'He (Chrétien) Doesn't Really Care'], . . . we've got punitively high rates of taxation."

Later in the same show, a caller named David asked Day if he could convince Canadians that his 11% flat tax, which he's already legislated in Alberta, or the Alliance plan for a 17% flat tax in Ottawa, won't lead to further spending cuts in education and other programs. David described it as "selling the well to pay for the farm. . . . Where is the money going to come from to invest more into the future economy?"

"A lot of people quite properly ask that question," said Day. "It's not just in Canada . . . [but] in every jurisdiction . . . where taxes are reduced, you see an invigorated economy, increased activity, both from the work-force and from the investors. And in fact what happens [is] you generate more revenues by more people working, but being taxed at a lower rate." Day went on to say that the flat-tax proposal would raise basic exemption levels to $10,000 for every person, which would take 1.9 million Cana-dians completely off the federal tax rolls. In Alberta alone, Day's flat tax means 132,000 low-income people won't have to pay any income tax at all.

Warming up to his favourite fiscal pitch, Day told David to "look at the results. The lowest unemployment rates in the country are in Alberta and Ontario, where low-income people, first of all, are paying less tax and in fact having jobs and able to get ahead." (Eighty-three percent of new job growth in Canada is coming from Alberta and Ontario, the two provinces that have cut taxes most radically. Lower taxes aren't the only reason, of course, but even critics of tax cutting concede they're a major factor.)

Really warming to his favourite subject, Day said, "This was also the case in 1961. When John F. Kennedy, a Democrat — a Democrat, not a Republican — significantly lowered personal income taxes, there was a huge uptake in terms of economic activity. When [Ronald] Reagan did it in 1981 as a Republican, we saw the same thing happen. Now there was also quite an increase in military spending through the 1980s that offset some of the gains." Day wrapped up his rant with the aforementioned Puerto Rico example, adding, "When tax dollars are being spent more respectfully, the taxpayers come to the surface. There is a huge under-ground economy right now in Canada. Economists and accountants say anywhere from 28 percent to 40 percent of the economy could be underground."

On March 26, 1997, Premier Ralph Klein unveiled his post-election cabi-net. Day was elevated from social services to the key post of treasurer, replacing the popular Jim Dinning. His predecessor had retired from pol-itics, but not before eliminating the provincial deficit by cutting $3 billion in government spending over the previous four years and leaving Day a $2.2-billion surplus to work with.

"The deficit dragon is dead and people are now thinking spending can just start again," said Day. "That's not going to be the case." Day brought with him a reputation as a fiscal and social hard-liner, having supported widespread welfare cuts in his previous portfolio and publicly backed Dinning's efforts in cutting spending elsewhere. Typically, he made no apologies. "If being a hard-liner means being careful with taxpayers' money, then yes, I'm going to be very careful." Day also announced plans to bring in legislation making it illegal for the provincial government to raise taxes without public approval in a referendum.

In politics, of course, the performance doesn't always match the script. Day got off to a rather inauspicious beginning. His first major announce-ment, on April Fool's Day, just one week into his new job, was to tell Albertans that another $15 million of their tax dollars was going towards an out-of-court settlement. The case in question was one of the lawsuits against the government stemming from the 1987 collapse of the Principal Group financial conglomerate, bringing to $130.5 million the total paid out by the province over that fiasco.

Day claimed the payment would save money in the long term: "It was simply to end this expensive legal process." The same day, he announced the province would swallow a $272.2-million debt owed by Millar Western Pulp Ltd. of Whitecourt, a town on the McLeod River about a hundred kilometres northwest of Edmonton. The province loaned the company $120 million in 1987, but in the ten years since had failed to collect a nickel in either interest or principal payments, allowing the debt to mount as unpaid interest compounded. Day announced that he'd accepted $27.8 million, or a paltry ten cents on the dollar, to free Millar from its debt to Albertans.

Day first floated his flat-tax idea on April 20, 1997, the day before deliv-ering his maiden budget. "Largely, we are governed by federal tax laws," he said. "But if we can get a good consensus across the country with the provinces, the federal government has said they are willing to allow some creative changes to happen. So I am willing to take up that challenge with them and look for ways they can change doing business that will help us as provinces." Even the opposition Alberta Liberals felt it was worth looking at, with Liberal treasury critic Gene Zwozdesky commenting, "The caution I would build in there is some kind of low-income threshold."

Day's budget was essentially a carbon copy of one tabled by Dinning on February 11, just before the provincial election was called. However, Day added $144 million to health spending, $91 million to education, and $68 million to advanced education. Day estimated government revenues would fall $2 billion, mainly because of declining oil prices, but still forecast a $154-million budget surplus. He also said he wanted to hear how Albertans would feel about one-time tax breaks, or "prosperity dividends," given that the province's shrinking net debt of $3.5 billion was due to be paid off entirely by 2005–06. He lamented the fact that Ontario Premier Mike Harris would implement his second round of income-tax cuts in July and thus overtake Alberta in having the lowest income tax. "Albertans need to know that Ontario's provincial income taxes will be lower than ours. We're still the lowest overall, but in this lane of the tax track, they'll be ahead." Opposition leader Grant Mitchell argued that more social spending was needed before taxes should be lowered, declaring that a shrinking net debt wasn't the best indicator that it was time for tax breaks. "The other indicators are whether you've got health care, education and responsibility to our communities and to people who are less fortunate taken care of before you consider tax reductions that won't help," he said.

Three days later, Day issued a correction to his budget after the Liberals found he'd made a $32-million error by not including interest owed by Alberta-Pacific Forest Industries (Al-Pac) on its $374-million government loan to build a pulp mill near Athabasca, north of Edmonton. "This is an accounting oversight I take full responsibility for," said Day. He subsequently announced that he'd asked the provincial auditor general to review all Alberta's outstanding loans and loan guarantees to make sure the debts were stated fully and in plain language.

In May Ontario's Harris announced plans to lower provincial income-tax rates to 45 percent of federal taxes in 1998 — the lowest in Canada, half a percentage point lower than Alberta's rate. Day again repeated his interprovincial competitive desire to keep Alberta's personal income taxes the lowest in Canada. "We'll be asking [Albertans how they feel about] bumping down personal income taxes even a percent or two."

By late August, Day announced that, because of strong oil and gas revenues, first-quarter results showed the province would vastly exceed its forecast budget surplus of $154 million, and likely hit $575 million by the end of the fiscal year. Day's original forecast had been criticized by many observers for being deliberately conservative in estimating revenues from the oil patch, so news that revenue was soaring hardly came as a surprise.

In September, Day announced the province was headed for a $1.2-billion surplus — nearly nine times his original budget estimate — much of it from stronger-than-expected sales of Crown leases and bonuses, rights to explore government land for oil and gas. In addition, personal income-tax revenue would jump by $33 million and corporate taxes by $17 million, thanks to the growth in employment and a generally buoyant economy. At that rate, he said, the net debt might be gone by 2000, "a wonderful millennium treat."

He defended his conservative budgetary estimates, saying that Tories prefer to err on the side of caution to avoid disappointments. "That's why we don't project wildly like some would like us to." Not to mention the fact that underestimating good news is a time-honoured tradition that allows politicians more opportunities to make happy-face announcements.

Liberal Opposition leader Grant Mitchell again called for more spending on health and education. "It's now beginning to hurt people," he said. Later that same day, responding to a work-to-rule campaign by Calgary public-school teachers seeking a 7% pay hike, Day announced an extra $31 million in overall education spending. "Albertans have told us education is a key area. It's a priority and that's why you see education being the first to enjoy . . . the prospects of us having a surplus beyond what we expected," said Day.

But just to show that he meant business in holding the line on government spending and cutting taxes, Day hired James Forrest, former director of the Alberta chapter of the Canadian Taxpayers Federation, as his executive assistant. He got into a dispute with the head of the Alberta Teachers' Association (ATA), however, when he told the *Calgary Herald* editorial board the government had never promised to restore the 5% wage rollbacks that public-sector workers had agreed to three years earlier to help the province balance its books. ATA president Bauni Mackay said Day's comments were "unfortunate" and an apparent attempt to "fan the flames" of a labour dispute with Calgary teachers. Day said, "Restraint is part of the way we'll live. This is a long-term way of life for the government of Alberta."

Over the Labour Day weekend, Day hosted Alberta's first-ever Growth Summit, inviting 102 representatives of industry, agriculture, the energy sector, government, social agencies, municipalities, schools, and hospitals to chart an economic course for Alberta to the year 2005. Before the summit began, however, he cautioned against expecting a government spending spree. "Our message going in is that this is not a spending summit. It's asking various sectors of the economy to project as far as ten years out how do we manage this good period of sustainable growth that we're in."

The summit pinpointed education as its main priority, followed in order by health and municipal infrastructure, with a lower priority placed on tax breaks and debt repayment. This prompted Ralph Klein to concede, "I would say there is some pressure to invest and to invest wisely." Day said that he too recognized the need to spend more to deal with Alberta's growing population. "We're in a time of very positive economic expansion. We've had as many people come to Alberta in the first six months of this year as we had in all of last year. We've got industry that wasn't there before. We've got heavy trucks pounding the roads that weren't there before."

This pressure to dip into the province's embarrassment of riches grew in October. It came not from the usual suspects, but from a gathering of a thousand rank-and-file Tories at the party's annual convention in Edmonton. Day acknowledged the pressure to shift from cost-cutting to spending, but said, "I don't think there is anyone saying don't spend an extra dime. I think there is a consensus that if we are going to be spending beyond the budget plans in place, it has to be intelligent, and the need has to be clearly recognized."

While most of the pressure was directed at loosening the fiscal strings of government, some sectors of the economy felt Day hadn't gone far enough in the other direction. In a December 30, 1997, article in the *Calgary Herald,* Fazil Mihlar, a senior policy analyst at the Fraser Institute, chided the Tory government for spending more per capita than four other provinces: Ontario, Manitoba, Saskatchewan, and Nova Scotia. "Meanwhile," wrote Mihlar, "Alberta is making no effort to reduce its $23 billion in gross debt. For this year, the cost of carrying this debt load is $1 billion. . . . Before considering any flurry of spending, the government should consider policy action that would bring tax relief to Albertans. If Alberta is to ensure greater economic prosperity, lowering taxes and paying down the gross debt once the net debt is eliminated would be the best policy."

Day ended the year by predicting a budget surplus of about $2.2 billion, nearly double his August projection. This was the fifth consecutive year in which Alberta enjoyed a budgetary surplus, again prompting teachers and other groups to demand increases in spending.

In January Day responded to the pressure, announcing a one-time extra infrastructure grant of $220 million for Alberta schools, municipalities, and highway projects. Schools got $100 million for more classrooms, new technology, and building repairs. Roads and other provincial infrastructure also got $100 million, with colleges and universities sharing $20 million for spending on new technology. Day had earlier announced an extra $40 million for hospital equipment and a $2-billion payment against Alberta's $16-billion debt.

In his February 12, 1998, budget — his second — Day said poor expectations for Alberta's critical oil-patch sector would cut $1.5 billion from provincial revenues, leaving an overall surplus of well below $1 billion. The expected US$1-per-barrel decline in the price of oil alone would cut $152 million in revenues. "There is a reduction in revenues and yes it is significant," said Day, "but our economy is still strong, very strong." Day predicted an overall provincial growth rate of 4 percent, down from the "phenomenal" 5.5 percent a year earlier. He expected a population increase of 52,000 people, the creation of 40,000 new jobs, and a dip in the unemployment rate to 5.5 percent from 6 percent. He said that crude-oil revenue was expected to drop by one-third to $644 million, placing it below lottery revenue for the first time. Natural gas was expected to produce $1.3 billion in royalty revenues, down from $1.6 billion.

Things weren't bleak enough, however, to dissuade Day from scrapping the province's machinery-and-equipment tax a year ahead of schedule, at a cost of $98 million. The tax was levied mainly against petrochemical and other petroleum-related companies with plants outside major cities. The revenues went for schools and municipal services. Day said the government would recoup that in other tax revenue, through increased economic activity. "Investment will actually increase and we'll end up bringing more money in taxes. We said, 'Show us the money.' They have." Within a year, tax revenue from petroleum-related industries actually did outstrip the special surtax.

In February, Day waded into the Liberal leadership contest, saying he was "startled" to hear that two of the leading candidates — including Nancy MacBeth, the former Tory cabinet minister who turned Liberal and won the contest — say they might reluctantly support a short-term deficit if the government faced plunging resource revenues. "The message that I've heard pretty clearly over the last few years is that Albertans are fed up with deficit financing and that's why we have a law in place that says deficits are illegal. So if anybody wants to change that situation they would have to break the law or repeal it."

Day set up a provincial tax-review commission in May, telling it to report back in the fall on whether the province's personal tax rate, already cut earlier in the year, should be cut even more. Day, a self-described tax-cutting hawk, left little doubt where he stood. Again he compared Alberta's tax rates to Ontario's, saying, "In terms of all taxes, we're still better off in Alberta." His comments came in the wake of an Ontario budget that cut the tax rate there to 40.5 percent of the federal income tax rate, from 45 percent, effective July 1.

Alberta's tax rate was currently 44 percent of the federal rate, cut from 45.5 percent in Day's February budget. Day said the average Alberta family with two children would still pay 18 percent less in total taxes, including health-care premiums, than a similar Ontario family, even with the Ontario tax cuts. That's mainly because Alberta is the only province without a sales tax. Ontario has a 8% sales tax, and most provinces have even higher sales taxes. In late June, Day was asked by the *Calgary Herald* editorial board what level he thought provincial personal income taxes should be at. "Call me a dreamer," he said. "Zero." Then he went on to caution, "I'm talking really long term."

He was also asked if he was jealous because Ontario's income-tax rate pushed Alberta into second place in that category. Day said, "A little." If he was jealous, it didn't last, because the same day that he talked about a zero income-tax rate, he announced that Alberta had knocked $2.6 billion off its debt, thanks to a record $2.73-billion surplus for the 1997–98 fiscal year, boasting, "It's a great time to be treasurer. It's a great time to be an Albertan." The increase over the projected $2.35-billion surplus came from higher-than-expected income-tax revenue plus an extra $33.5 million in profits from video lottery terminals, which had risen in the previous year to $518 million.

Day made his first visit to New York that June, ringing the bell at the New York Stock Exchange to start the day's trading. He was there to sell the so-called Alberta Advantage — a combination of low taxes, great economic opportunities, and skilled workers — to a group of powerful investment firms, including J.P. Morgan, Morgan Stanley, Merrill Lynch, and utilities giant General Electric Investment Corporation.

In October, the special taxation committee that he had appointed earlier in the year released its report and, as expected, recommended a $500-million tax cut and a flat income tax for Albertans, long one of Day's pet projects. At a subsequent Tory convention in Banff in November, Ralph Klein announced that he'd asked Day to measure the economic impact of further tax cuts. This came after the majority of the 1,100 convention delegates called for a tax cut ahead of saving money in the province's Heritage Trust Fund.

Klein said that Day would begin public consultation on the future direction of government fiscal policy, which could include tax cuts or increased spending on health and education. He denied that the consultations would simply duplicate the efforts of last year's Growth Summit — although that was the stated purpose of the summit — because the "dynamics" had changed in light of the tax committee's proposal. "Stockwell's consultation is making doubly sure we're still on the right track," said Klein.

There was no doubt as he headed into the "consultations" about which track Day was riding. In the federal arena, Reform Party leader Preston Manning and others, including Day, had already begun what was then known as the United Alternative. This process — which ultimately evolved into the Canadian Alliance — was an effort to stop the two conservative parties, Reform and the Progressive Conservatives, from splitting the vote and allowing the Liberals to win. The need for a united front was deemed particularly urgent in Ontario, where, largely because of vote-splitting, Prime Minister Jean Chrétien and his party had won all but two of the province's seats in the last federal election.

It was at the provincial Tory convention in Banff that the 55-year-old Klein made it clear he was not interested in running for leadership of the United Alternative. "The United Alternative is not a party, it's a movement," said Klein. "I'm not going to be their leader. I'm going to take Alberta into the next century."

Certainly most Alberta Tories were pleased about that, including Day. But for the ambitious politician, considered by many to be Klein's logical successor, the premier's decision to stay on as leader must have made him consider his options. With the next election not expected until 2001, Klein, assuming he won — a pretty sure bet in Alberta — would still be premier in 2005, when Alberta would celebrate its centennial.

In late November, Day announced that unstable oil prices, the devalued Canadian dollar, and higher social spending had slowed Alberta's revenues, although he was still expecting a budget surplus of nearly $250 million for 1998–99. With a built-in "cushion" of $420 million, Day said he still expected to make a $667-million payment on the accumulated provincial debt of $25.5 billion, which included unfunded pension liabilities of $5.5 billion. "Healthy growth in the past year, despite global uncertainty, means our income projections are ahead of target," said Day as he released the province's second-quarter financial report. "Our economic strengths are attracting record numbers of people from other provinces."

Day suffered one of those minor embarrassments politicians hate. He told reporters that with 77,000 people coming into Alberta last year, at a cost in government services of $5,000, that's an extra $375 million.

"Actually," a reporter pointed out, "it's an extra $385 million."

Day shrugged. "What's $10 million between friends?"

In a November 29 interview with Canadian Press in Edmonton, Day said Alberta had become Canada's "go-to" province, attracting job-seekers and job-makers from coast to coast. There were some concerns that the province would be a victim of its own success. "Alberta's arms are open," he said, "but the streets aren't paved with gold. They're paved with hard sweat."

Day said Alberta had taken in 122,690 people from Canada and abroad over the previous four years, on top of about 91,000 more births than deaths, jumping Alberta's population by about 7 percent to 2.9 million. The majority of the migrants — 40 percent — came from British Columbia, followed by Ontario, with 15 percent, and Newfoundland, with 11 percent. While entrepreneurs were opening businesses of all sizes, Day conceded that "some people are having difficulties. The province is handling the situation, but it is not without its challenges."

In Calgary, the 0.6% apartment vacancy rate was the lowest in Canada for the second year in a row, with rents rising an average of 11.5 percent. In Edmonton, vacancies dropped from 4.9 percent in 1997 to 1.8 percent. New arrivals, Day said, even if they had a job and could afford rent, often couldn't find a place to rent. Up to 45 percent of people living in temporary emergency shelters had jobs. On the plus side, housing starts, which had languished at 15,000 a year since the mid 1980s, shot up to nearly 24,000 in 1997 and were expected to top 27,500 in 1998. The number of students grew by 2 percent, and Education Minister Gary Mar said, "Some of our schools have a utilization rate of 104 percent."

In spite of Alberta's difficulties, Day said, things were generally good. "I've talked to various ministers in other provinces and they would love to have our problems." Even so, Day announced on December 11 that provincial cabinet ministers had been told to scale back their spending expectations in anticipation of a revenue nose-dive in 1999. "We are obviously not going to be tabling a deficit budget in February 1999," he said. "But will there be a significant surplus? I don't think so."

In mid-February, Klein and all the premiers — except Quebec's Lucien Bouchard — signed a social union deal with Ottawa, giving the provinces more say in setting objectives and national standards before the federal government introduced new social programs. But Day told the *National Post* he wasn't thrilled with it. "It's like the song says, 'You can't always get what you want.' No we didn't get everything. There [were] some gains made, but I think there are more improvements to pursue. I would be encouraging people to press on for more improvement."

Despite the agreement, Day felt that Ottawa continued to have a condescending attitude toward the provinces. "I think it is an attitude of a federal government which says we always know best, all the time, what is best for you immature, undeveloped provinces, and you need to be quiet and listen to us. It is that overriding attitude that stifles some of the positive solutions that I think are there to make this a more vibrant country."

In late February, Day, having again understated Alberta's surplus, announced that a jump in personal income-tax revenues, due to population growth and a strong economy, had put an extra $766 million into the provincial coffers, upping the surplus to $672 million, despite low world oil prices. "People are voting with their feet and their U-Haul trailers," he said. "They think Alberta is a place with a future."

In his March 12 good-news budget Day mapped out a historic plan to cut the province adrift from the federal tax system. He also announced a variety of tax cuts and nearly $2 billion in new spending, including $935 million for health, $568 million for education, $209 million for advanced education, and $160 million for social services, all over the next three years. Day also did away with two deficit-elimination surtaxes.

But the key proposal, which attracted journalists from across the country, was Day's plan for a flat tax of 11 percent on taxable income by January 1, 2002, along with a boost in personal exemptions designed to save the average Alberta family up to $1,200 a year and knock some 80,000 Albertans off the tax rolls. Day said the measures were aimed at easing the burden, simplifying the tax system, and eliminating "tax-bracket creep." He added, "I'm saying to Ottawa: 'Sit up and take notice of what we're doing, and if it works, why don't you do it?'" — speaking more like a man priming for national office than a provincial treasurer. *National Post* columnist Andrew Coyne wrote, "Whatever it means for Stockwell Day's career prospects, the Alberta Treasurer's recent budget is of major economic and political significance for the rest of us. In one move, it has pushed tax reform — radical, root-and-branch reform — squarely onto the national agenda. That's tax reform, note, not tax reduction."

Indeed, in late May, Ontario Premier Mike Harris announced at an election campaign stop that he planned to follow Alberta's lead and divorce his province from Ottawa's tax system. As for Liberal leader Nancy MacBeth, her response to Day's budget was "What's being sustained here? Alberta's future or Stockwell Day's?"

In April, Day was scrambling to comply with a deadline imposed by the Supreme Court of Canada the previous October, after a ruling that some of the $1.2 billion collected by the province in user fees was an unconstitutional tax. The court had ruled that probate fees in Ontario were actually a form of taxation, because the amount charged was disproportionate to the service rendered. Alberta had intervened in the case.

Day said that about eight hundred fees set by cabinet order would be approved by the legislature in order to comply with the ruling. "The Supreme Court said you can charge anything you want or whatever you want, but if it is significantly going beyond cost recovery then you need to put it in statute — bring it in the legislature." He promised to review every fee to determine "which are legitimate and which should be lowered."

In July, Ottawa gave Pratt & Whitney Canada a $154-million Technology Partnership Canada (TPC) "risk-sharing" grant just four months after the World Trade Organization ruled that TPC funding for Bombardier Inc.'s regional jet was a hidden export subsidy. With the question of offering subsidies to big business heating up again, Day said, "It's a very attractive and powerful forum as a politician to stand up and get on the front page by saying: 'Look what I did.' But it's a fading dream that turns into a nightmare. Governments have an amazing ability to pick losers rather than winners." Alberta picked a whole string of losers in the early 1990s, losing billions of dollars through poor investments, which culminated in the province's 1995 Business Limitation Act outlawing direct subsidies to private enterprise. Instead of direct subsidies, said Day, governments should offer lower taxes, reduced red tape, and enhanced infrastructure to attract firms or encourage expansion of existing companies.

But then, Day didn't have to announce the location of a new plant in order to gain yet another spate of good-news headlines. On July 25, he announced what he called the "rosy news" that higher crude-oil prices had sparked Alberta's surplus to surge to $1.5 billion. The Fiscal Responsibilities Act, passed by the province in the spring of 1998, requires Alberta to devote 75 percent of any surplus toward paying down its debt. "It means we will have more money to handle growth pressures. All in all, Alberta is the place to live and pursue your hopes and dreams," he said.

Heading into the annual premiers' conference in Quebec City, Day, echoing the laments of premiers and provincial treasurers past, was openly pitching the idea that Ottawa should cut income taxes by 20 percent over five years and overhaul the federal tax system to return more of the money to the provinces. "The federal government has been taking more revenue from the provinces and it is the provinces that are trying to handle the pressures of growth," he said. "We then have to go hat-in-hand begging for some of our money back to fund health care and education."

In August, he warned the oil patch that rising gasoline prices could spur calls for price controls. "If consumers think the price is going up unfairly to them, it creates an opportunity for those who want to leap in with price controls of some kind," he said, explaining that he was giving the industry a "heads-up" after opposition calls for government intervention on gasoline prices. Announcing the first-quarter budget results in September, Day said Alberta had hiked program spending by $260 million and was thinking about changing its legislated debt-payment plan to make more money available for roads and sewers. Once again, Day's surplus forecasts turned out to have been wildly understated, the actual surplus coming in at $1.992 billion, more than triple the $617 million forecast in the spring budget, thanks again mostly to ballooning energy and income-tax revenues. About half the new money, $256 million, was earmarked for education, health, and fighting forest fires. Another $13 million was spent to help new children's services authorities during their first year of operation. That gave Alberta an average surplus of $1.7 billion every year since 1994–95, for six straight budgets. And while oil and gas remained key elements, Alberta's economy had diversified considerably during those years. The previous year, for example, despite a 40% drop in oil and gas revenues, the overall economy still grew by 3.7 percent.

Speaking at a conference of Alberta municipal leaders in October, Day acknowledged the province suffered a shortage of affordable housing but had no intention of getting back into the business of building them. Instead, Day said, he was looking at rate subsidies for the needy, particularly for seniors' housing, but he called on local government to "partner" with the private sector to build up the housing stock.

Later that month, Day took his fiscal gospel on the road, telling a group of students at McGill University that his "dream scenario" would be to eliminate provincial income tax within 15 years, preferably with a referendum around the time of the hundredth anniversary of income taxes in Canada. Income taxes were brought in by Ottawa as a temporary measure in 1917 to help pay the costs of the Great War. While Day and his colleagues may not like the tax, personal income-tax revenue increased by 64 percent, more than 10 percent a year, during the first six years of the Klein government.

Returning from meeting bond dealers and investment bankers in New York a few days later, Day complained that Ottawa's failure to tackle the $576-billion national debt was discouraging foreign investment in Canada and hurting all the provinces, including Alberta. "We're still under the federal umbrella," he told the *Edmonton Journal*'s Norm Ovenden. "When they [investors] see holes in the umbrella, rain falls on the investments. Everywhere we went, the question of government spending at the federal level had a significant bearing on the investment discussions. We were surprised at the amount of attention they pay to that."

Day and other ministers were accused by Liberal MLA Colleen Soetart of "talking out of both sides of their mouths," because they drove high-priced cars at the taxpayers' expense. Day had the cabinet's most lavish vehicle, a 1999 Toyota 4Runner worth $37,800. "Don't talk about how Albertans need to tighten their belts, or run a health-care system where hip replacement surgery takes 12 months, and then drive around in a $37,000 car," said Soetart.

Day ended the year pretty much the way he had begun it, by making easy headlines. Emerging from a meeting with experts in public and private pensions, he said Alberta could set up its own pension program if the federal government didn't fast-track proposed reforms to the Canada Pension Plan. "We are not making any announcement that we are pulling out of the plan," said Day. "We are asking if there are other options."

In Ottawa, Finance Minister Paul Martin said Day's concerns were "perfectly reasonable." But, he added, "My understanding is we're waiting for the Alberta officials to put down papers exactly explaining their position, which they have not yet done. We and the provinces have said we're certainly prepared to examine them." Shortly after that, however, Martin did announce a series of CPP reforms responding to concerns expressed by the provinces and other stakeholders. This prompted the *Edmonton Journal* to editorialize that Day "should savour victory" and forget about opting out of CPP.

Following a meeting with his friends at the Canadian Taxpayers Federation, Day announced he was considering a 20% cut in health-care premiums as one of several measures to return a $3-billion surplus to Albertans. Alberta families paid $816 a year, while the individual fee was $408. Day had already announced he was considering further tax cuts, and he removed the 8% deficit-elimination surtax on incomes of more than $47,000 a year. He also talked about lowering the province's fuel tax of nine cents a litre.

But a day later, Day redirected his public musings, saying Albertans might not see any tax cuts after all, because the extra money could be used to help pay off the debt. "That way the interest savings continue forever, year to year to year," he said. Craig Chandler, national president of the Progressive Group for Independent Business, told the *Calgary Herald* that Day "shouldn't have opened his mouth in the first place and got our hopes up. This was coffee shop talk where the regular, everyday Albertan was talking about getting a $100 rebate cheque. . . . I think a lot of people are going to be very disappointed that they were teased. And that's exactly how they're going to perceive it. It was an outright lie to the public." But Kevin Gregor, incoming president of the Calgary Chamber of Commerce, supported Day. "So long as Alberta retains the lowest income tax regime in the country, then paying down the debt isn't a bad idea."

In February 2000, Day appointed a blue-ribbon committee to review business taxes, such as corporate income tax and the hotel-room tax, to ensure Alberta could be competitive on a global scale. "The message has to be that we're running ahead of everybody else, and this is the place to be thinking of not only keeping your business, but moving to," said Day, noting that Alberta collects more corporate income tax as a percentage of gross domestic product than New York, Michigan, Ohio, California, Texas, and Indiana. The Liberals called the panel a "Valentine's Day bonbon" for corporations. "I'm amazed at how many times this Treasurer can talk about tax relief without doing anything," said Liberal MLA Howard Sapers.

Ten days later, Day certainly did do something about taxes and spending, surprising both his political friends and foes alike. First, he again promoted his 11% single-tax plan, slated to begin in 2001. But he also went on a major spending spree, promising to hire 2,200 more teachers and teaching assistants and 2,400 nurses and other health-care workers, although he dipped into a $3.5-billion federal trust fund to do it. He also offered taxpayers a slight break, with greater tax relief in the future and cutting $60 million worth of user fees. Day's $17.7-billion spending package included $482 million more for health and $266 million for education.

The new budget represented a $1.6-billion boost over the previous year, the largest single spending hike since Peter Lougheed's 1985–86 budget. Despite all that spending, however, Day announced $3.2 billion would go to pay down the $14.1-billion provincial debt — making Alberta the only province to own more than it owes — and still enjoy a $713-million surplus.

Fiscal conservatives reacted to Day's budget with dismay. *Calgary Herald* editorial-page editor Peter Stockland, for example, wrote, "The current incarnation of the Klein caucus has apparently kidnapped the real Stockwell Day and hidden him in some attic behind great-grandpa's steamer trunks. How else to explain the treasurer's defence of last week's beer-gut provincial budget? Only an imposter for Day could have extolled . . . a plan to have Alberta belching $17.7 billion in government spending for 2000/2001 fiscal year. . . . The original Day brought an auctioneer's understanding of impulse spending to the Klein cabinet table. He understood, from his former career, that once bidding and spending begin in earnest, competitive instincts take over and dollars begin to flow without regard for real value."

In his federal budget a few days later, Paul Martin surprised just about everybody by announcing that he, like Day, was getting rid of "bracket creep." His income-tax cuts forced Day to go back to the drawing board when they turned Alberta's 11% single-rate tax into a tax increase. Economists discovered middle-class Albertans would be better off by several hundred dollars a year with the old tax system than with the new one. This prompted Day, on March 16, when he formally introduced his long-awaited bill to impose the country's first flat tax, to acknowledge that he might have to cut his single-tax rate to 10 percent or increase the basic exemptions. "Albertans will be the first Canadians who will be able to work overtime or become upwardly mobile or work harder without being punished with a greater tax rate," said Day, explaining his decision to uncouple Alberta's tax system from the federal system.

Day was outraged, however, that Martin's budget excluded oil, gas, and mining companies from Ottawa's highly touted plan to slash corporate income-tax rates from 28 percent to 21 percent. "We're talking about hundreds of millions of dollars here," he said. "It does not look as if the oil and gas companies are being treated as fairly as the other business sectors in Canada." The only exception was the energy sector, but Ottawa said it already received a 7% resource allowance, giving it an effective tax load of 21 percent. But David MacInnis, a spokesman for the Canadian Association of Petroleum Producers, said giving other industries that advantage would mean market investment in oil would wither in favour of red-hot sectors such as high-tech stocks. Oil prices, at US$30.42 a barrel, were at their highest price in nine years, but the industry was languishing on the stock market. MacInnis maintained that less investment meant less oil and gas exploration and fewer jobs and spin-offs. "As an industry, this is going to make us less competitive. Investors are already staying away from oil and gas stocks."

While Day generally receives high marks for his years as treasurer, not everybody agrees. Rich Vivone, publisher of the Alberta newsletter *Insight into Government,* says Day is "a terrific stump speaker with a great sense of humour. He has a first-rate, congenial personality, but as a politician he's vastly overrated."

Vivone, an executive assistant in the 1980s to the Tory education minister, says, "Much of his success as treasurer is a matter of timing. He's provincial treasurer when there's so much money flowing into this province they don't know what to do with it. It's pretty easy to be treasurer now. We haven't seen Stock in a situation where you have to make a tough decision, where there are two equally valid competing values and you've got to choose one. That's the real test of leadership. We haven't seen that with him."

There's some truth to that, of course, but it's hardly Day's fault that times are good. Oil and gas were also flowing during the previous Getty government, for example, yet the Tories racked up enormous debts by following a strategy of profligate spending. In Ontario, legendary Premier Bill Davis ruled Canada's wealthiest province throughout the 1970s and into the 1980s during a time of remarkable prosperity, but never once managed to present a balanced budget. And Liberal prime ministers Lester Pearson and Pierre Trudeau placed the country deep in hock even though most of their terms occurred during good times. When Brian Mulroney took over from the Liberals in 1984, the country faced a $160-billion debt. After ten years of so-called "restraint," the debt was $489 billion. The current Liberal government began with a $489-billion debt and, despite record tax revenues, pumped it up to $620 billion by 1997 before starting to pay it down. Even so, it remains at an astronomical $577 billion.

There's little doubt that after several years of preaching of the tax-cut message by Alberta and Ontario Conservatives and the Reform Party, the political agenda has changed dramatically, not only for the federal Liberals, but for every province in the country, whatever its political stripe.

On March 28, for example, Bernard Lord's Conservative New Brunswick government jumped into the tax-cutting game with a 5% drop in personal income taxes. The next day, Saskatchewan's NDP government copied Day's lead by unveiling a revamped tax structure that cut taxes, ended bracket creep, and de-linked the provincial tax from its federal counterpart. Finance Minister Eric Cline admitted it was an attempt to stay competitive with neighbouring Alberta. "The status quo is not an option," he said. "We must move forward."

Which, of course, is precisely what Day did that same month, when he stepped down as Alberta treasurer and announced he was running for leadership of the Canadian Alliance.

7

LOOKING EAST

—

Day was there at the beginning — which, for all practical purposes, was a Reform Party assembly on May 29, 1998, in London, Ontario, where Preston Manning first convinced the assembled believers to explore the controversial notion of forming a united alternative to defeat the governing Liberals.

Day was the keynote luncheon speaker at that meeting, flown in and put up at a hotel at Reform expense.

He had certainly earned his invitation. As Alberta's labour minister in April 1996, Day openly threw his support in the next federal election behind Reform, despite the fact that his boss, Premier Ralph Klein, was a public booster of then federal Tory leader Jean Charest.

"I support in principle most of the Reform Party's policies in terms of being fiscally and socially conservative," said Day, adding that he had even talked to Reform MPs about merging their party with the federal

Tories in order to win the election.

A few weeks later, Day announced he would be chairman and moderator of Winds of Change, a conference organized by conservative columnist David Frum, to be held in Calgary in late May. The conference, which afforded Day significant national media exposure, brought together a host of Canada's leading conservative thinkers to propose solutions to the split in the right-of-centre vote, which, if not repaired, would result in yet another Liberal government. In many ways, that conference kick-started the movement towards a right-of-centre, anti-Liberal coalition, moving the issue from the political backrooms onto the public stage.

In a subsequent interview looking back on the Winds of Change conference, Day said, "The intent was to get the winds of discussion blowing and stir things up. It did that. It resulted in the present ongoing discussion." Day feels a precedent had been set earlier in the last century when the Progressives and the Conservatives merged to form the current PC party. "Maybe it's time for the Conservative Reformers."

By the spring of 1998, despite his impressive success at the polls, Preston Manning understood better than most that Reform was only the latest in a series of protest parties. Political organizations would ride in from the West intent on lassoing the power-brokers of Central Canada and forcing them to pay more attention to western needs and aspirations. These movements had had mixed results — although most enjoyed temporary successes — but none had achieved more than Manning's Reform Party, which won 52 seats in 1993 and then 60 in 1997, enough to form the official Opposition.

Despite that impressive record, however, Manning knew that in some respects political parties, even successful ones, are like businesses. If they don't continue to grow, they'll wither and die. He realized, after his second failed attempt to corral Ontario voters (where his vote total actually fell substantially), that if his movement was ever to achieve anything beyond the status of a historical asterisk or another notch on the belt of western protest, he had to expand his base.

That is why Reform gathered in London that May weekend, and why it was significant, even then, that of all the provincial politicians in the land, only one was invited to speak — Stockwell Day.

All this unite-the-right talk from Day and others certainly helped Manning sell his gospel of a united alternative. After two years of patiently lobbying Reform members about the concept, Manning went to the May 1998 assembly in London and got what he wanted: permission from the party's rank and file to begin exploring the notion of some sort of coalition among disparate conservative groups. His ultimate goals were, first, winning seats in Ontario, and second, ultimately defeating the dreaded Liberals.

As for Day, he got even more valuable exposure within the conservative movement. He was regularly touted at the time as logical successor to Ralph Klein as premier of Alberta, having served as acting premier on occasion during Klein's absence. Day delivered what was for him a typical, high-energy speech, without using any notes. It featured a lengthy passage in French on the theme that Canadians are not *maîtres chez nous* (masters in our own house) because Ottawa has forgotten it is supposed to be the servant of the people, not their master.

The *Calgary Herald* reported that the speech, given the federal nature of the assembly, "got some tongues wagging about whether he [Day] has federal aspirations." There was speculation he was looking at Manning's job, or at whatever job might ultimately flow from the notion of a united alternative.

Day denied any personal interest in seeking federal political office — well, sort of. "My heart is in Alberta, and other imaginations are not in my head. I am totally focussed on Alberta and trying to keep that budget in line."

But one senior Reform official told the *Herald* afterwards, "He's running for something. The question is, which job is he running for?"

Day may not have been technically running for anything at the time, but he was secretly involved with a powerful group of federal and provincial Conservatives. They were negotiating with senior Reform strategists, hoping to draft plans to create a conservative coalition or even a new party, to unite the forces of conservatism against the federal Liberals.

Day was widely quoted on the initiative in September, when news of the ongoing negotiations leaked out. For several months Day had been actively exploring the idea with Ontario Transportation Minister Tony Clement; Klein's long-time senior aide, Rod Love; senior federal Tory fundraiser Bob Dechert, the leader of a high-level group of Toronto-area Tories called the Blue Committee; and Brian Mulroney's former principal secretary, Peter White. Rick Anderson, Manning's senior adviser, was the Reform leader's representative at the meetings.

The group's immediate goal was the formation of an advisory committee to organize a national convention for the United Alternative (UA) campaign in February 1999, as well as drafting the movement's political blueprint.

"We're an informal group of individuals right now," said Day. "We should know in the next couple of weeks if something formal can be pulled together. I don't know if it can be achieved. I hope it can. I don't want another five to ten years of free-spending Liberal rule."

Reform had hoped to formally announce the membership of the advisory committee by that time, but because of philosophical differences between some of the federal Conservatives and the Reformers, the announcement was delayed. Day ended up co-chairing the national advisory committee along with Ontario Transportation Minister Tony Clement, in preparation for the inaugural United Alternative convention, slated for Ottawa in mid-February 1999.

While this process was unfolding in the fall of 1998, the Conservatives were involved in a leadership race of their own to replace Jean Charest, who had left the party in March to become Quebec Liberal leader. Day had predicted that when Charest left, the chances of uniting federal Conservatives and Reformers would improve. "I think it opens the possibility," he said, noting that Charest was "absolutely opposed" to the idea. "I think now this will open things up — at least for some discussion to take place." What Day didn't know — couldn't know, of course — was that former prime minister Joe Clark would become the once-and-future leader of the Tories, and close off any avenues for mutual discussion.

When Charest quit, the once-mighty Progressive Conservative Party still had 90,000 card-carrying members, about four times what it has now. Clark ended up winning the job after a run-off with David Orchard, a radical Saskatchewan farmer and anti-free-trade crusader. Clark had earlier dismissed Orchard as a "tourist" in the Conservative Party, but later welcomed Orchard into the party's inner circle after he, Clark, began losing the support of most Tories of any consequence.

Rather than slow the movement towards a coalition, the election of Clark — who vociferously rejected all overtures from Manning to explore a united alternative — caused many right-of-centre Conservatives to abandon the party for the new conservative movement. What began as a trickle in 1998 has since escalated into a flood.

Even middle-of-the-road Conservative Premier Gary Filmon of Manitoba met with Manning in late October. He said later he favoured looking at a possible partnership at the national level, although he'd stay on the sidelines. Filmon felt that the movement must come from the grassroots, not from the political elite. "It has to come from the people themselves."

Five days later, Ralph Klein upset Clark and the federal Tory establishment by agreeing to deliver the keynote address at the upcoming United Alternative convention and suggesting the Tories were "on life support." "I don't think we can have two parties on the right, fighting each other," said Klein. "I do think there needs to be some kind of amalgamation or coalition."

In Ontario, Premier Mike Harris, Klein's eastern counterpart, kept his own counsel, although several of his cabinet and caucus colleagues were openly endorsing Manning's efforts. In Alberta essentially the same people voted Reform federally and Conservative provincially. Harris, however, had to deal with a reality in which Reform voters and Conservative voters were quite different animals. Historically, Ontario's Conservative voters have tended to split into two major camps, the blue, or more right-of-centre, contingent — more prominent in the smaller cities and rural areas — and the pink Tories, or Clarkites, found more in Toronto and other major cities. In winning two consecutive majorities in Ontario, Harris had relied on support from the entire conservative spectrum. He wasn't about to openly endorse any one of the groups, although he made no effort to discourage his own people from taking sides.

Clark again haughtily dismissed Manning's invitation to attend the planned UA convention, and continued to refuse to even discuss the issue. Ontario Solicitor General Bob Runciman, definitely a blue Tory, offered the prescient prediction that Clark "may find himself on the outside looking in. I think it is regrettable." Ontario Tory MPP Bill Murdoch added, "Clark is totally wrong. He loses, again, by ignoring this."

As for Clark, he told the annual Tory convention in Banff that "the unhappy, inescapable reality is that any new organization that looks like Reform or walks like Reform will not be successful in Ontario and Quebec and in Atlantic Canada." Clark claimed he had a plan to attract disenchanted Tories back to the party, although he refused to give details. If he did have a plan it's still not obvious what it may have been.

Former Reform MP Stephen Harper, who left the party to take over the National Citizens' Coalition, said that if Clark "takes an objective look at this he should see that he might be able to do something for the country by getting involved. He certainly isn't going to do anything by simply refusing to even consider it." But refuse he did.

In January, the United Alternative committee, which Day co-chaired with Clement, floated a bizarre trial balloon — which went *poof* shortly after it was let loose — calling for a so-called confederal party made up of five strong regional blocs, each with its own elected leader. Supposedly, the party would give Canada's regions more power over central decision-making, but it's difficult to see how a party with one leader and five powerful deputy leaders, plus five different regional organizations, could ever make a decision on anything.

The committee offered some more-sensible options for consideration at the conference. They included creating a new party from scratch, uniting behind an existing party like Reform or the Tories, forming a loose coalition, or formally merging the two conservative parties (an exceedingly unlikely option, given Clark's continued opposition to the whole unite-the-right idea).

In a provocative keynote address to more than 1,500 delegates at the Ottawa Congress Centre in February 1999, Klein — a former Liberal — said the newly reconstituted party should do two things: recognize Quebec's unique character, and stay away from social issues such as abortion and homosexuality. These two pieces of advice, if heeded, would pretty well make it another Liberal Party.

Klein, a fiscal conservative but definitely not a social conservative, argued, "We cannot, as those who adhere to conservative philosophy, declare ourselves to be the party of minimum interference in the everyday lives of everyday Canadians, and then propose to interfere in the most personal of all decisions — those decisions that are matters of conscience, those issues that present a moral dilemma, those things of so personal a nature that the decision becomes one between an individual and his or her God."

Klein received what was generously described as "polite applause" for his criticisms of social conservatism, which contrasted sharply with the standing ovation he received when he said, "We urgently need to fix the maddening trend towards judge-made law."

In order to avoid public disputes over contentious social issues, the convention organizers opted to obfuscate, preferring to promote generic policies such as support for families and for individual freedom and law and order. All those against families, freedom, and law and order, please rise!

Reform MP Jason Kenney, a strong social conservative who would become Day's senior aide in the leadership contest, said it was decided to postpone debate on those issues until after UA delegates had reached agreement on broad principles. "Sooner or later we are going to have to cross that bridge, but I think that we don't want to create unnecessary points of disagreement prematurely."

In an interview with the *National Post* at the time, Day argued that the best practical solution for defeating the Liberals, or at least denying them a majority, is for Reformers and Conservatives to co-operate in running candidates in Ontario. He said a new party would not succeed unless it had broad support among grassroots Tories as well as Reformers. "I'm not actually convinced it's the best option." In the long run, he said, a merger would be the best option, but that wasn't possible in the short term because of Clark's determination to fight the idea. Clark was risking having the "grand old [Tory] party become a rump party . . . I would appeal to Joe to truly do something great for the country and his party, which he dearly loves, and think about the possibility of a merger, but that's remote."

Going into the weekend convention, Day strongly endorsed Manning as the best choice to lead a new right-wing party. Critics continue to claim that the convention was just a meeting of Reformers using the United Alternative name as an alias. This was not the case. Of the 1,512 delegates at the three-day convention, 861, or just 57 percent, were Reformers. Only 62 delegates registered from Quebec, most of them what organizers called "soft nationalists," while the rest, just over 40 percent, were Tories — not a bad turnout from a party whose leader was vehemently opposed to any accommodation with Reform.

At the time of the convention, a COMPAS research poll suggested that 53 percent of Canadians would support a new party discernibly to the right of the governing Liberals, up from 36 percent in a similar survey five months earlier. Despite his own numbers, Conrad Winn of COMPAS said that Canadians "are not looking for an alternative to the Liberals. They are not angry at the Liberals." Yet at the same time, Winn said anger over high taxes could lead Canadians to support Reform. Jean-Marc Léger, president of the polling firm Léger & Léger, had thought going into the conference that the United Alternative idea was five years ahead of its time. Predicting a third consecutive Liberal mandate in the next election, Léger said the United Alternative "is an answer to a wish that Canadians have not yet formulated."

Late Saturday afternoon, before Manning pleaded with the delegates to "unite from the heart," Day delivered a rousing leadership-style speech of his own. Day's "pulpit persona" was described in a *Calgary Herald* feature at the time as "one part true believer, one part stand-up comedian," knowing "how to inspire supporters, encourage doubters and get everyone feeling good." Well-known Calgary oil baron Jim Gray, a veteran Progressive Conservative who watched the convention, described Day's oration as a "Clint Eastwood speech" that wowed the delegates. In a subsequent *Calgary Herald* interview, Gray said Day's main challenge was overcoming the stigma of being a radical. He said Day has obviously learned a lot on that score by watching Manning, because his speeches at the UA convention and the Reform convention a year before in London, Ontario, were generally moderate in tone and content. "He has started to build his image with those speeches," said Gray. Calgary MLA Mark Hlady, a Day supporter, reflected on what had become the so-called common wisdom: that Day will need to speak a different language if he wants to connect with sceptical Ontario voters. "He has to temper his own personal views if he wants to be a leader," said Hlady.

Day's speaking style clearly outshone the plodding, pedantic Manning, placing him in a position to run for the leadership of a new party himself. For sure, Manning's speech was warmly received, but Day's was a big hit, eliciting at least a dozen standing ovations. The *Calgary Herald* reported that "the more engaging Day turned heads with a personal off-the-cuff address mixing humour, fluent French, and ringing criticism of the federal government that left delegates impressed."

How impressed? Well, Tory Senator Gerry St. Germain, a former Mulroney minister and national Tory party president, said, "He's a real presentable candidate." Edmonton Reformer Peter Schalin, remembering Day from 30 years earlier as a hippie with a beard and long flowing hair, said, "Awesome. I'm very impressed. What I like about Stock is he speaks from his heart. He's very passionate and he has integrity."

Thunder Bay delegate Sandy Smith said Day's achievements as Alberta treasurer have spread to Ontario. "He obviously has the knowledge and the know-how to make Canada work." And Brian Stecyk of Spruce Grove, Alberta, said Day "says it the way he sees it. There's nothing phony about him."

After the convention, Ralph Klein, who had ruled out any chance he'd be a leadership candidate, made no secret of the fact that he'd support Day should his treasurer decide to run. "I would encourage him to get involved in whatever way he can," said Klein. "I have a lot of . . . respect for Stockwell." Day remained coy about his own intentions, but insisted the new party must not be simply a born-again Reform party. "This is by no means a Reform-driven thing," he said. "There was substantial support from senior federal Tories as well as young Tories. . . . This dream of PCs and Reformers working together is going to become a reality, and a nightmare for the Liberals." As for his own leadership plans, Day said, "I'm very flattered people would suggest it. That fragrance has been in the air, but I'm not inhaling."

Perhaps the biggest surprise of the convention was Manning's invitation to Quebec separatist Rodrique Biron to deliver a keynote speech, a transparent — but apparently unsuccessful — attempt to build support for the movement in Quebec. Many citizens of that province remember Manning's 1997 campaign ads, featuring Quebec political leaders with diagonal lines drawn through their faces, which may have played well with constituents in some places but enraged Quebecers. While both Biron and the equally radical Jean Allaire received sustained applause for their formal speeches, many Reformers were privately grumbling about

Manning's decision to invite avowed separatists to participate in the convention. "We were really upset when Mulroney brought all those separatists into his caucus and cabinet," complained one Reform MP, "and now here we are trying to cater to them just to beat the Liberals. I didn't like that and I wasn't the only one. But nobody wants to say that out loud because it would create more trouble than it's worth."

One significant result of the convention was a palpable momentum among many delegates towards the idea that Manning, while genuinely respected and admired, was not the best choice to lead a "new" party. "Without a change at the top, this will be the same old, same old — the Reform Party in a new suit," said Mike Heenan, a delegate from Brampton who a year later was working in Day's campaign. Anthony Wallbank of Woodstock, Ontario, told Manning he should step aside for the sake of the new party and the country.

Al MacDermid, a student at the University of Western Ontario, approached Day after his speech and said, "Great speech. I want to know if you want to be the driver of the bus."

Day said he couldn't imagine seeking the leadership, although he did not rule it out completely. MacDermid said to a reporter, "If we're going to have a new movement, we have to have new leadership." And senior Ontario Tory Peter White, a member of the UA steering committee and a close associate of Brian Mulroney and media mogul Conrad Black, said, "A new party would certainly need a new leader." For all that, however, Manning made it clear from the outset that if there was to be a new party, he'd be seeking its leadership.

In the end, the delegates voted to create "a new party for a new century" to replace the Tory and Reform parties. Manning declared, "I again make it absolutely clear the door is open for the leadership of the federal Conservative Party to reflect on what has happened here this weekend." Joe Clark didn't reflect for long. "I have no interest in a new party," he said. "I intend to make my party work."

While the creation of a new party was the preferred option, with 665 votes, or 55 percent of the delegates, the other three options had varying levels of support. Some 273 delegates said they'd rather start co-operation between the two parties at the riding level by fielding joint candidates, especially in Ontario, while 252 wanted to unite behind one of the existing parties. Just 33 delegates opted for a merger of two or more parties.

The vote meant that the 21-member steering committee — Reformers, Tories, and other non-Liberal activists — had the authority to begin planning a founding convention for the new party, with a leadership convention to follow. Two days later, Day resigned from the committee, saying he needed all his time to concentrate on the upcoming provincial budget. Many saw his resignation as making it easier for him to mount a leadership campaign.

"I have no plans other than to focus on Alberta and the job the premier has given me," said Day. "I have indicated to the steering committee that I'm delighted the train has left the station and that my work there is done."

In fact, Day spent considerable time over the next year laying the groundwork for a possible run at the leadership. He hadn't decided he'd go for it, but he understood that if he did run, a successful leadership bid needs money, organizers, and support, things that can't be built up overnight.

Not all Reformers were pleased with the convention results, some fearing that the new coalition would mean watering down Reform policies, particularly the thorny social-conservative policies, in order to attract more centrist Conservatives to the movement. Outspoken Reform MP Myron Thompson of Wild Rose, Alberta, predicted that his riding would turn down the idea. "Don't expect me to compromise a great deal on my principles and values." Nobody did.

After being warned by Klein to avoid the social issues — and subsequently being given the same caution by several pollsters — the convention delegates skirted around specific social policy issues by approving a series of broad resolutions calling for support of personal freedom, the family, the justice system, immigration, and the role of government. They did support a policy to "recognize the family as the essential building block for a healthy society." Some more liberal delegates saw a plot even in that motherhood resolution, underscoring the difficulties inherent in attempting to reconcile social conservatives and social liberals in a common cause. Derek Vanstone, 27, told the *Ottawa Citizen* he voted against it because he detected a veiled anti-abortion reference in the resolution's preamble, which said the party would recognize "that all human beings possess the fundamental human rights of life, freedom and the right to own property."

In March, Day was one of the main roasters, along with Preston Manning and *Alberta Report* publisher Link Byfield, at a Calgary rally and roast honouring the tenth anniversary of the election of Reform's highly respected deputy leader, Deborah Grey, to Parliament.

On the night of the roast, Manning had to defend himself again over the contents of a 20-page report on the Ottawa convention that he had written and mailed to more than 70,000 party members. The report, alas, demonstrated two unfortunate sides of Manning's character: first, that he can be petty and spiteful, and second, that he can be spooked, as he had obviously been by Day's performance. The report is brimming with countless references to Manning and five pictures of him, but despite general acknowledgement that Day's speech stole the show, just one oblique reference is made to him. Not only was Day's speaking style well received, but he had the critical task of presenting the option of forming a new party to the convention delegates. Many of them conceded that Day's forceful delivery helped nullify the opposition towards it.

In his report, Manning hailed Reform MP John Reynolds's "rousing presentation" and former Tory candidate Gordon Gilchrest's "thoughtful speech." When it came to Day, he had apparently run out of adjectives, making only a passing reference to the treasurer "who spoke in favour of creating a new party." A front-page *Edmonton Journal* headline declared, "Manning Leaves Day in the Dark."

When confronted by reporters at the Grey roast, Manning dismissed the headline as "just nonsense, absolute nonsense. . . . There was no slight intended there at all. We couldn't put everybody's picture in there. I wouldn't start interpreting things on the basis of pictures." He added, "Stockwell made an excellent contribution. . . ."

While Day was at the microphone roasting Grey, he joked that for once he wasn't worried about his words coming back to haunt him because, after all, nothing he said would get written up in the Reform brochure anyway. Manning, returning the joke, said, "I don't know how we left his picture out. I mean, we have it hanging on the wall of our bedroom."

Despite their public display of jocularity, however, several Day supporters bitterly complained. Day himself said, "Preston and I are great friends and I have nothing but admiration for him." He acknowledged that pressure was mounting on him to seek the leadership, but repeated, "My focus is on Alberta. I've still got some things I want to do here yet, so that's where I'm at." But Reform's Mark McConnell, president of the Edmonton Southwest riding association, said Day would be "absolutely terrific" as leader. "He would be more marketable in Ontario. He's fluently bilingual. He has a sense of humour. And he has a track record."

In April, Day agreed to be the keynote speaker at a fundraising event for Ontario Transportation Minister Tony Clement, another key player with Day on the United Alternative steering committee. Five hundred federal and provincial Tories paid $150 each to hear Day speak, many of those Ontario Tories anxious to assess his credentials as leadership material. Surprisingly, Day did not mention the United Alternative at all in his speech. Afterwards he told the *Edmonton Journal,* "People know my point of view. People will sit back, weigh out the pros and cons and whatever decision they make, we'll live with." He said it wasn't his job to sell the concept any more. "I give individuals more credit than that. You don't need politicians trying to rub their noses in one particular view or another. They know the facts of life and I think they'll make a good decision."

In June, Reform members voted just 60.5 percent in favour of continuing to explore the United Alternative process. It wasn't permission to fold Reform into something else, only to explore the idea. The relatively close vote prompted Day to warn UA organizers to "proceed with caution . . . I think the message is to proceed carefully. Clearly, 60 per cent is satisfying, but when you have 40 per cent saying no, that is a message of caution. I think people are in touch enough with the grassroots of the party to know that, as they move ahead, they need to move ahead carefully so that you bring along those who are concerned about the direction."

Day, who had just announced that Alberta's credit rating had been boosted by Moody's Investors Service of New York to AA1, the highest possible rating, said, "People are presuming I am looking or considering the leadership of this, but I am not." He claimed there was a growing desire among Conservatives to work with Reform to defeat the Liberals, and that the movement had enough positive momentum to succeed. In Ontario, Clement said the vote would mean a "rigorous push" within the Conservative ranks to recruit members. "There are many people who want to move forward," he said.

Ralph Klein, who once described Reform as "a pimple on an elephant's butt," made it clear — again — that he would not run for leader of a new right-of-centre party. Barry Cooper, a political science professor at the University of Calgary, told the *National Post,* "I really don't think Ralph gives a damn about Ottawa. I think he's quite happy to stay in Alberta and do what he has set out to do. Though it certainly may increase the temptation for Stockwell Day. I think he'll see it as an attractive next step, whereas I think Ralph's attractive next step will be retirement."

Klein publicly called on Joe Clark to stop opposing the UA effort, calling it "the truly viable alternative to the Liberals." He said Day would be "a marvellous candidate" to lead the new party. In Manitoba, then Premier Gary Filmon offered lukewarm support, saying, "I think it's healthy to have a strong alternative to the Liberals, but the success of the United Alternative will depend on its leaders and its policies."

Throughout the fall and into the early part of the new century, Day busied himself with his duties as Alberta's treasurer. But he still found time to quietly build a campaign team and appear at partisan events across the country, exposing his platform talents to a broad variety of potential UA supporters, and getting ready for a speech at the UA convention slated for January 27 to 29 in Ottawa.

Not everybody was happy. Reform MP Dick Harris, a vocal UA opponent, declared in early January that he might challenge Manning for the leadership of the Reform Party. Separatist Rodrique Biron quit the UA steering committee in a huff because Reform decided to support Jean Chrétien's so-called clarity bill, which laid out the terms for possible separation. In response to growing criticism from within, Manning issued a surprise ultimatum on January 7, 2000, in a bluntly worded letter to the party's 70,000 members, vowing to resign as leader if they rejected his UA initiative. Manning said he was "increasingly convinced" the UA was the only chance "for achieving a Reform-oriented government and for implementing the principles for which we have fought so long." He remarked later that "the Reform VCR has no rewind button. There is just a play button and a fast-forward."

After receiving Manning's letter, two dissident Reform MPs announced they were now going to support the UA initiative. But a day later, Gee Tsang, Reform chairman and the party's highest-ranking grassroots official, resigned over what he called a plot by Manning loyalists to seize control and limit debate at the upcoming convention. He accused Manning's allies of wanting to strip him of power because he refused to publicly endorse the UA. "I have been a very honest person. I have been neutral and impartial," the Saskatchewan Reformer said. "I have never said I am pro-UA. And, [on] the other hand, I have never said I am against UA. I have always maintained a neutral, unbiased position, but that apparently makes somebody uncomfortable." Manning's allies in Reform responded to the charges by accusing Tsang, who had been highly regarded by everyone until then, of being incompetent and politically dangerous.

Manning got a bit carried away on January 17 when he predicted that western separatism, which never was a major force and had been dormant for years, could increase if the UA failed. Shortly before the convention, the National Citizens' Coalition released an Environics poll showing that Reformers were badly split over Manning's initiative. The poll of four hundred Reform voters showed that 48 percent favoured the UA, with 47 percent opposed. But Reform pollster André Turcotte said his polls showed that 75 percent of Reformers and 71 percent of Conservative supporters would move to a United Alternative.

Day's ongoing influence on the UA was demonstrated again when Reform MP Monte Solberg and Toronto accountant Kevyn Nightingale, co-chairs of the UA policy committee, released their proposal for a single income-tax rate, the centrepiece of the policy debate at the founding UA convention. The proposal for a single federal-tax rate of 17 percent was modelled on Day's innovative 11% flat-tax rate in Alberta, scheduled to come into effect in January 2001. Day says it will shave $600 million from provincial revenues and save a typical family $1,200 a year in provincial taxes.

"There's no doubt that what Stockwell Day and the Alberta government have proposed is a great example for us," said Solberg, his party's finance critic. "It's an inspiration. We think it's tremendous they're leaders in this area."

As delegates to the three-day UA convention arrived in Ottawa on January 26, Amanda Marshall's "I Believe in You" was being pumped through the loudspeakers and volunteers were busy slapping "Yes, 4-UA" stickers on everything that moved. A resolution to create a new political coalition was easily passed by the 1,100 delegates, who had paid $500 for the privilege of attending. But Manning still had to sell the package to his party members when the convention would become an all-Reform event later in the weekend.

The UA policy proposals, rather grandly entitled "Declaration of Policy," had been mailed earlier to all the delegates. "What Canadians want is results," said Manning. "I don't think they care a lot about the internal politics of the party, and this is all about getting the 150 members you need in the Parliament to get taxes down and heal health care and democratize federal institutions."

Some Reformers still worried that their beliefs would be sacrificed on the altar of winning more seats. Senior Ontario backroom Tory Tom Long, the convention co-chair — who would later become a leadership candidate himself — confirmed the worst fears of some doubters when he said it was important to "re-brand" Reform policies to appeal to a broader range of people, particularly in Ontario.

Pollster André Turcotte argued that the UA could win more support than the Tories and Reform combined, slashing a 33-percentage-point lead for the Liberals in Ontario to 11 points. "It's very difficult for people to do that," he said. "It's a lot easier if we give them something brand new and fresh to join." Reform MP Lee Morrison called that "bloody nonsense." He thought Reform was fine the way it was. "If we have saleable policies, and I think we do, what's the point of putting it in a different package? To the average Ontario voter, a policy is a policy is a policy. Why have we spent a year eviscerating ourselves to come up with the same policies that we had all along?"

In presenting his flat-tax plan to the convention — where delegates ultimately approved it — Solberg said the plan could save Canadian families $5,000 on their annual tax bills. "It would give everyone a big tax break and in doing that, unburdens the economy and allows it to create a lot more jobs and prosperity." It would also remove about 1.9 million of Canada's poorest from the tax rolls altogether, he said. Critics say the plan would give the biggest break to rich people and make middle-income Canadians shoulder the largest proportion of the burden. Finance Minister Paul Martin attacked the plan immediately, saying "the vast majority of the benefit goes to the wealthy Canadians," and that "the proportion of taxes under the circumstance that would be borne by middle-income Canadians would go up. In our view, that is simply unfair."

As for Day, he delivered another energetic, 45-minute speech to the

1,100 delegates, without notes. He said it didn't matter who led the attack against the Chrétien Liberals in the next election, but it made "common sense" for him to support the UA just as it did for Reform Party members. He received two standing ovations. Day also had some kind words to say about Preston Manning. "I've got a two-word phrase for principle that gives me confidence those principles won't be lost," he said. "That two-word phrase is 'Preston Manning.' Preston is the only politician I know who has said, 'I want the leadership of that and I want everybody who wants to, to challenge me.'"

Day, sounding like a man trying to reach out to all factions of the coalition, also offered an olive branch to those Reformers who were unhappy with the process. "I would be remiss if I didn't take a moment to share with our Reform friends who have concern with this whole movement. Your views are important and they need to be listened to. That is number one. And they need to be respectfully listened to." Day touched on a host of issues ranging from the environment and the treatment of aboriginal people to taxation, immigration, and what he portrayed as the lost art of governments listening to the people and representing their views.

"Let's remember those principles. Let's remember that, if you're like I am, you are probably weary of government MPs coming to your riding and saying, 'We, the government.' Whatever happened to 'We, the people'? That's what we're talking about here, and respecting that."

Day also demonstrated what *Maclean's* magazine described as his "almost Trudeau-esque eye for the photo op" at one point during a lull in the proceedings. Standing onstage, he suddenly whipped off his suit jacket and shirt, revealing a T-shirt with the sleeves rolled up, James Dean–style. "Wrapping his tie around his head," wrote *Maclean's*, "he feigned a few martial arts kicks, which naturally earned him a prominent spot in many of the nation's major newspapers the following morning." It also helped to convey the notion that Day is not only younger than Manning, but physically fit and brimming with energy, not a bad image for a politician to promote.

In addition to approving the flat tax, the delegates moved into controversial new territory by supporting a motion recognizing Canada's two official languages and official bilingualism, a sharp departure from traditional Reform policy. They also approved Alberta-style balanced-budget legislation, a tougher line against crime and punishment, elimination of financial support for multiculturalism, an end to both farm subsidies and affirmative action programs, denial of recognition to same-sex couples, immediate deportation of illegal immigrants, more police on the streets, elimination of the 5% high-income surtax, an increase of RRSP limits to $16,500, reduction of capital gains and corporate taxes, downsizing of government, and fewer regulations for business.

Before anything official happened, however, Manning had to demonstrate that he enjoyed the continued confidence of his party, in a leadership review scheduled for the Reform portion of the weekend convention. If he passed that test — which he did, with a solid 75% vote — the next step was a mail-in vote by all Reform members on adoption of the constitution and policy framework of the new party. A two-thirds majority was needed and the party members had until March 17 to submit their ballots. The results would be announced at yet another gathering, this time in Calgary, on March 25. If the initiative was approved, then the final step in the process would be a Canadian Alliance leadership convention in late June, also in Calgary.

Day wasn't the only potential leader who performed well at the Ottawa convention. Ontario Tory strategist Tom Long, a former Mulroney adviser and a key component of Mike Harris's electoral victories, received five standing ovations and elevated himself as a leadership possibility with a fierce attack on Joe Clark.

"We have to be direct. If you are a conservative and you really want change in Ottawa, Joe Clark is not your answer, we are," he proclaimed. "For years, Joe Clark has lectured conservatives, tiresomely lectured conservatives about the unfashionability and unsalability of their beliefs. He has spent his entire career looking to forge alliances with literally any group but conservatives and he has no meaningful record of accomplishment in promoting the things conservatives care about. The reason for this is quite simple: Joe Clark is not a conservative."

Long's and Clark's mutually hostile feelings date back to the early 1980s, when Long was one of a group of Brian Mulroney loyalists working hard to undermine Clark's leadership of the party. They were ultimately successful in getting rid of Clark when Mulroney defeated him for the party leadership in 1983 and went on to win two consecutive majority governments. However, at the end of his career Mulroney was one of this country's most hated political leaders.

After the convention, party officials met with embarrassment over the official name of their new party, the Canadian Conservative Reform Alliance party, or CCRAP for short. NDP MP Lorne Nystrom mused whether politicians would be allowed to use the acronym in Parliament. "Would that be unparliamentary?" he asked. Reform officials insist that the name ends with "Alliance" and that the P for "party" is not part of the formal name. The party was to be known as the Canadian Alliance. Perhaps — but expect to hear references in the next election to the "CRAP" party from its critics.

Preston Manning had every right to feel good about the success of his initiative. But he quickly turned one of his finer moments into a not-so-fine moment when he again displayed the unattractive, autocratic side of his nature for all to see. Just two days after the convention, Manning fired his high-profile House leader, Randy White, a Vancouver-area MP who was widely respected both in the party and within the House of Commons generally. White's "crime" was that, while he ultimately supported Manning's Alliance initiative at the conference (he had remained neutral until then), he also spoke openly on television and to newspaper reporters about the need for strong challengers against Manning in the spring leadership campaign. Manning himself had consistently been saying he hoped the leadership race would attract strong candidates — particularly an Ontario candidate — but apparently what was fine for him to say was verboten for his number-three man. "I refused to get down and kiss the ring," said White, telling reporters, "I'll be looking elsewhere [beyond Manning] for leadership." He's backing Day.

Other Reformers accused Manning of using a "scorched-earth policy" to convince members to support his initiative. Saskatchewan Reform MP Allan Kerpan said Manning had not told a caucus meeting that he was bouncing White. "He [White] was the best House leader we ever had. He worked damn hard at it. I am shocked, but not surprised. I don't know what the reasons are. I'm getting tired of this stuff," said Kerpan.

Manning wasted little time after the convention in launching his cross-country campaign to convince Reformers to approve the new Canadian Alliance. He left Ottawa on February 8 and didn't return until the February 28 budget was announced. A good chunk of the Reform caucus was out doing the same thing. MP Bob Mills, who, like Day, represents Red Deer, said he planned to attend 11 town hall meetings over the next month as Reform members received their ballots. "I always feel guilty when I miss one day here [in Ottawa]. I try not to," said Mills. "But if we don't make the Canadian Alliance happen, we are not going to be a strong opposition to the Liberals."

8

CHARGING IN

When Day arrived back in Alberta following the Alliance convention, he was asked again if he was interested in becoming leader of the new party.

He didn't exactly say no.

"The problem is if someone asks you if you'll ever go into federal politics and if you say never, and then down the road if you ever did, then somebody will come up with a tape or a piece of video saying, 'Look, you said never, and now you did.'"

Anyway, said Day, he was too busy just then preparing for his February 24 provincial budget. "I'm working every hour of the day to make sure we have the best budget in the country."

As for Ralph Klein, he took the time to say, "Stock would be a good leader, yes. Stock is a very good treasurer and if he demonstrates the same qualities as treasurer through a leadership of some party or another, I don't know what it would be, yes I think he would be a good leader."

At the same time, the first stirrings of a "draft-Day" movement were beginning to surface. Day said he didn't have time at the moment to "return faxes, e-mails or phone calls on the [leadership] issue." Reform MP Jason Kenney, a senior Manning confidant and the first MP Manning turned to in 1997 to help him launch the United Alternative project, told the *Calgary Herald*, "There are any number of people urging him [Day] to run for the leadership. Nothing is definite yet, but I've been hearing a lot of rumours there may be something definite pretty soon."

Kenney was in a position to know. He and Klein's long-time senior adviser, Rod Love, were the main strategists behind the draft-Day movement. Both are now arguably the two most powerful members of Day's leadership team.

Day did take the time on March 9 to hold a news conference to say he would decide his leadership plans within three weeks, leaving little doubt that if the Reform members voted to form the Alliance, he would run against Manning for the top job. Day's statement came after the campaign to draft Day received more than 10,000 visits to its Web site, www.draftstockday.com, on the first day. "One more day and we'll have enough to fill the Saddledome," quipped spokesman Pierre Poilievre. Even better, he said, "We've had tons of comments from areas where the Reform Party has not, in the past, been successful breaking in, like Quebec, the Maritimes, and Ontario." By the end of the first week alone, the site had received 40,000 hits.

Key public endorsements came from Ralph Klein and from Edmonton Reform MP Ian McClelland — considered to be on the left of the Reform caucus, and father of a gay son. McClelland said Day had the skills to appeal to both ends of the political spectrum. "He's got the attributes that will make him successful. He's got some baggage that he will have to get over, but I think he has the skills to get over that. For him to leave a very cosy job here in Alberta, to take that on, it will be a person answering a call and an obligation, and people that do that should be respected. I am going to be in his corner." Klein said, "I have always said that Stockwell Day, in my mind, would make a tremendous leader. I believe that in order for the new conservative party to rejuvenate itself, it needs a new leader with a new tone and a new style."

A day earlier, Jason Kenney, Reform's revenue critic and senior organizer, made public his allegiance to Day — the first major defection from Manning's inner circle. Kenney said his decision to call for a new leader was the most difficult of his political life. He said Day's bilingualism "is an absolute necessity if we are serious about not just picking up a handful of seats in Ontario, but forming a majority government." To those who argue that Day's connections to the religious right will hurt his national appeal, Kenney said, "People are respectful of the fact he has a moral compass and aren't afraid of the fact that he goes to church on Sunday." He said Day has "tremendous growth potential. I suspect that most people who are drawn to Preston Manning's leadership are probably already in the Reform Party. I think it would be fair to infer that his growth potential is more limited."

In an open letter to the party, Kenney said that Manning could not make a breakthrough in Ontario, a view echoed by the colourful Reform MP Myron Thompson of Wild Rose, Alberta, who said he decided to support Day after much internal soul-searching. "Realizing that Preston deserves it — he wrote the book — but I don't think he can carry Ontario, so my support will be for Stockwell. The way I read Ontario is, they will vote for Stock."

Alberta Children's Services Minister Iris Evans said that tears flowed among her colleagues when Day confirmed his plans to seek federal office. "The premier said some nice things, and everybody applauded," she said. "Then when the premier was leaving, Stock stood up and they hugged each other. The premier looked over Stock's shoulder, and he had watery eyes, like we all did. It's because he's family. It was a very emotional moment this morning."

In announcing the unofficial start of his campaign, which was broadcast nationally on CBC Newsworld, Day showed another strength to his candidacy that the other leadership hopefuls don't have — his ability to speak French. Chantal Hebert, the *Toronto Star's* national affairs columnist, whose ideology is far removed from Day's, nonetheless wrote that, "It is a rare day in Alberta when a politician scores more of a hit with an answer to a question in French than to those in English. And yet that's what happened . . . when . . . Day switched to French to sketch out his decision to seek the leadership of the future Canadian Alliance. . . ." Newsworld was caught without simultaneous translation but, Hebert wrote, "It doesn't matter. The main point was that he was able to respond in fluent French, a feat Manning has yet to achieve despite weeks of French immersion lessons. . . . Like it or not, a federal leader with no French is like a canoeist without a paddle."

Hebert described Day's French as "rusty but still good for the road. While his verbs need brushing up, there is enough fluency to assume he would quickly grow more comfortable if he were, as federal leaders tend to be, exposed to French on a daily basis."

A week later, Eric Duhaime, a former political adviser to Bloc Québécois leader Gilles Duceppe, said that Day's mixture of keen political antennae and charisma would not only sell in Ontario but would translate into Quebec seats as well. Duhaime, who acted as a liaison between Quebec and English Canada for the Bloc, said Day is the closest he's seen in an English-Canadian politician to what he called "Quebec's vision of federalism." He said Day's ability to switch back and forth between English and French would siphon votes from the Bloc and the Liberals in Quebec. Rodrique Biron, a former Union Nationale party leader, called Day "a real provincialist." Biron, who was on the UA steering committee until quitting over Manning's support of the clarity bill, said, "Stockwell Day respects me as a Quebecer, and as a sovereigntist, and that's very important. The best point for Day in Quebec is his firm will to respect provincial jurisdiction."

In a post-budget visit to the *Calgary Herald* editorial board, Day said that Alberta's conservative approach to politics and government finances

would be an easy sell to the rest of the country. "The small 'c' conservative message that I talk about when I'm [in Ontario] — and I don't hide
anything about the fiscal side or the socially conservative side — it
resonates," said Day. "I find audiences there receive me just as well as
audiences here."

Curiously, Day said he planned to stay on as provincial treasurer if he
challenged Manning for the Alliance leadership, noting that Pierre
Trudeau stayed on as justice minister while he ran for the Liberal leadership in 1968. "It's very common." Not in Klein's Alberta — the premier
said if Day ran he'd have to step down for the duration of the campaign,
in the same way Klein and other ministers did when they ran for the job
after Don Getty retired in 1992.

In a move clearly calculated to overshadow Day's televised news conference, Manning told more than 150 people at an Empire Club luncheon
in Toronto that he would step down as official Opposition leader in the
Commons to concentrate on the Alliance leadership, if Reformers voted to
create it. This move was seen by many as yet another sign that Manning
understood he was in tough against Day. A further indication of the
potential strength of a federal election campaign led by Day came in
Ottawa, when federal Liberals gave journalists an eight-page list of so-
called "gaffes" committed by Day during his 13 years in office. It was
essentially a collection of controversial statements that Liberals and others
consider politically incorrect. If they weren't worried about Day, you won-
der why they would go to so much trouble attempting to belittle him.

A poll of 547 people by TeleResearch Inc. of Edmonton, commissioned
by the Draft Stockwell Day movement, suggested that 43 percent of
Ontario provincial Tories supported Day as leader, compared to just 9 percent for Manning. But of Alberta Reformers, 58 percent supported
Manning, compared to 40 percent for Day.

Two weeks later, an Angus Reid poll, done for Calgary television station
CFCN, found that Day and Manning were in a virtual dead heat for
support in Alberta, each man garnering 45 percent support from voters

should they lead the Alliance in a federal election. An editorial in the *Red Deer Advocate*, Day's hometown newspaper but often not a big booster, concluded this was bad news for Manning. "Both men are best known in Alberta because that's where their political roots are. But Manning founded the Reform Party and took it from ground zero into the official Opposition in a decade. Manning is also much better known personally here than in other parts of the country, and he comes across in person much more effectively than he does on television. If there's any place where you might think he [Manning] would have an advantage, it's Alberta. The fact that Day is running even with him in the Angus Reid poll is a real boost for his [Day's] campaign."

The day after he launched his unofficial leadership campaign, Day headed for Fortress Ontario, in symbolic recognition of where the real battle will be fought in both the leadership race and the next federal election. Day told about a hundred young Ontario Tories that federal Conservatives had to leave aside their old, emotional attachments and join the new Canadian Alliance if they hoped to defeat the Liberals. "There is a growing dissatisfaction for what is at the federal level," he said. "The system itself is creating dissatisfaction and discouragement." He called the billion-dollar "fiasco" in the federal human resources development department as "just the tip of an iceberg that has punctured the hull of the Liberal *Titanic* and as that ship takes on water, we're seeing disarray on the decks of management." Day said his social policy "is built on people having freedom of expression. People want to see less government in their face. Less government on their backs. That covers all areas of life."

One man who said he would be happy to see Day win the Alliance leadership was Prime Minister Jean Chrétien. On the eve of a raucous Liberal convention where the pro-Martin and pro-Chrétien camps were openly fighting, Chrétien said of Day, "I think I can beat him. It's going to be a debate on ideology. He's an extreme conservative, fine, and I am not. The debate in Reform is who will be more right wing than the other. That's great, because Canada is not like that."

But Liberal pollster Michael Marzolini added a word of caution, characterizing Reform as an "iceberg party" that is underestimated between elections but can sneak up during campaigns. "A lot of what I'll be talking about [at the Liberal convention] will be not underestimating the opponents," Marzolini told Canadian Press. "Their percentage level may not be all that high between elections but it tends to increase during elections because people are looking for alternatives to shop around with — the public wants options."

Two days before the results of the vote by rank-and-file Reformers were announced, Yellowhead MP Cliff Breitkreuz, a founding member of Reform, announced he was supporting Day because he believed Manning couldn't win in Ontario. "In 1993 we elected one guy in Ontario. In 1997 we went down, and lost the guy we had, and didn't elect any members. That's two kicks for Manning. He didn't even maintain a base, and that's the most pragmatic reason we have to look at someone else, and I think Stockwell Day can certainly improve on that."

While all this furious activity was going on in Alberta, the other provinces weren't exactly silent. In Ontario, former Reform candidate Joe Peschisolido, a Toronto lawyer, announced he was a candidate. British Columbia Reform MP Keith Martin, a medical doctor who is seen as a moderate on social issues but a hawk on more private funding of health care, said he'd jump in if he could round up enough financial backing.

Martin, who practiced emergency medicine before entering politics in 1993, argues that the country would be better off if Ottawa amended the Canada Health Act to allow a full-blown private system. "Not a single nickel of the taxpayers' money should go into the private sector," he told the *National Post*. "All of the tax dollars goes into the public system. The private system will support the public system. The rich will subsidize the poor. If it doesn't happen there is never going to be enough money from taxpayers to government to pay for all that we ask for. Our demand will continue to outstrip the supply of money we have. The only people who are going to get hurt are the poor and the middle class." He said Canadian politicians are so afraid of negative public reaction to "two-tier medicine" they're ignoring the fact our system is increasingly being funded by private sources. "It is a total myth to say that we don't have a two-tiered system. We have a multi-tiered system."

But a bigger story was just beginning to unfold at Queen's Park, where the Ontario Tories were desperately seeking a candidate. They had hoped that either Tom Long or Tony Clement would run. When they declined, the Tories turned to a little-known junior cabinet minister, Frank Klees. Still, it was felt that, with the backing of Long and the rest of the Toronto-based Blue Committee, the 49-year-old, unilingual Klees could make a respectable showing. That too was good news for Day, since one of the main reasons they wanted to field somebody was to make sure Manning couldn't garner enough votes to win the leadership on the first ballot. The Ontario Tory establishment has generally believed since the outset that, while many have respect for him, Manning cannot overcome his hayseed image and western twang and win seats in Ontario for the Alliance. Klees had conceded publicly that he was interested, but was holding off making a final decision pending the outcome of his fundraising efforts. We would be hearing more of Klees very soon.

For his part, Jean Chrétien was still going on about how Day's "right-wing views" won't sell in Quebec. Chrétien said Day "isn't better than . . . Manning. Very right-wing politicians in Quebec don't go very far." Day said he had received "a very positive endorsement out of Quebec and maybe that's why the prime minister appears to be a little bit afraid. Last week, he said day after day that he was not afraid of Stockwell Day, and yet he keeps talking about it." Jason Kenney said Chrétien's comments showed "who Chrétien is most worried about, and that's Stock Day. The Liberals know that a bilingual leader who has lived across the country, and is young and articulate with experience in government, like Stock Day, is their biggest threat. And that's exactly why Chrétien is saying what he is."

In the meantime, about four hundred eager Reformers and Conservatives gathered at Calgary's Metropolitan Centre on March 25. Manning, standing in front of a huge Canadian flag, announced on national television that 91.9 percent of Reform's rank and file had agreed to fold their party into the new Alliance. Of the 73,437 ballots mailed out, 48,838, or 65.5 percent of eligible voters, were mailed back. "I can't say how pleased I am," a beaming Manning said, to the cheers of the crowd. The vote, a personal victory for Manning after three tough years of selling the idea across the country, meant that the Reform Party Manning built 13 years earlier was now dead — except for its name, which the Alliance continues to control.

Among the raucous crowd, people were already wearing buttons that said "Preston!" while others wore "Run Stock Run." In the lobby, party officials were selling Reform memorabilia, everything from golf balls and tees to Frisbees, pens, pins, mugs, key chains, and embroidered shirts.

"I'm looking at the Alliance producing the next prime minister of Canada and I think the country is waiting for a prime minister with ideas," said Manning, "someone who's able to get people to work together to solve large numbers of problems. I'm ready for that job." Manning said later he still hoped that Clark would look at the results and join with the Alliance. No chance — not only did Clark reject the invitation, he quickly announced he was going to fight the party's use of the word "Conservative" in its formal name.

Day, who said he would run for an Alliance seat in the next federal election whether he won the leadership or not, entered the hall to the cheers and chants of his supporters. "I'm committed to the Canadian Alliance for the long term," he said. "What we've got here is a new movement. Frankly it has become a tidal wave."

He called the vote "the launch of something historic. It's going to spread across the country," and pledged to run a campaign on issues and priorities while avoiding personal infighting among the candidates.

Frank Klees told reporters that he was the only one with experience on the ground in Ontario. "If we don't win substantial seats in Ontario, we will not form a government. It's for a pragmatic assessment of who can deliver the votes in the next federal election."

The day after the vote, the Alliance national executive met at a downtown Calgary hotel to hammer out the leadership contest rules. It unveiled its new logo — a stylized green C and A — via a slick video that Canadians will be seeing a lot of. There would be no spending limits — Day and Manning both estimated it would take about $1 million to run a full campaign — and all candidates had to post a $25,000 refundable deposit and submit with their nomination papers 300 signatures from 30 ridings in five provinces. The party membership list would be made available to all candidates just as soon as they were officially recognized. The leadership vote was set for June 24 in Calgary, a one-member-one-vote mail-in. If there was no clear winner on the first ballot, a second would be held on July 8, but no new memberships could be sold between the two ballots.

Some of the outward harmony quickly disappeared during the all-day session. For one thing, Day's supporters were convinced — with good cause — that Manning had deliberately delayed announcing the vote totals until it was too late for Day to follow him on national television. Nor were Manning's officials, doing everything they could to give their man the edge, anxious to guarantee immediate access to updated party membership lists.

The fear was that Manning, in his role as leader, already had the access. "I am concerned about that, and we would want immediate access to the list," said Jason Kenney, Day's senior organizer. "Any candidate who ponies up the $25,000 deposit . . . should be walking out of the office with the full membership list within a matter of minutes." The Alliance co-president claimed that Manning "does not have direct access to that list," but he warned that other candidates could face some "administrative delays" before receiving their copies.

Supporters for both Day and Klees fought and lost against the decision to cut off membership sales one week prior to the June 24 vote and between ballots, if it came to that. The decision was seen as an advantage for Manning who, Kenney said, "has a 12-year head start." Manning dismissed their concerns, saying, "If people will try to find there is some-thing wrong, this is not going to be a positive exercise." Easy for him to say, since all the disputes went his way.

Manning scheduled his formal campaign launch for March 27 in Calgary. Day, who said he would step down as provincial treasurer, flew to Vancouver for a speech and an interview on CKNW radio with Rafe Mair, the country's most listened-to talk-show host. Day planned to kick off his official campaign in Red Deer the next day, then head off on a whirlwind cross-Canada tour to Barrie, London, Toronto, and Montreal, finishing in Halifax at the end of the week.

Besides Kenney, Day's team featured Rod Love, a major backroom strategist in Alberta; policy adviser Ken Boessenkool, who specializes in economics and worked for two years with the C.D. Howe Institute; and hot-shot, bilingual media coordinator Line Maheux, who had worked for Manning for more than three years and was also a former communica-tions director for Ontario Premier Mike Harris. Maheux said she agonized over which candidate to work for, but ultimately chose the Day team. Why? "I want to win," she said.

Rafe Mair, who has a well-deserved reputation for asking direct ques-tions and demanding direct answers, spent the first few minutes of the interview on constitutional matters. Then he asked Day, who wanted to talk about the economy, a question about abortion. Did he, Mair asked, as a fundamentalist Christian, "consider abortion a sin, and would you have a referendum on abortion if you were prime minister?"

Day said that "about 50 percent of Canadians . . . take a pro-life view" — which is arguable, depending upon how you define pro-life — adding that the debate over abortion in Alberta concerned tax-funded abortions, not whether abortions should be legal or not. "Those of us taking the pro-life position that tax-funded abortion should not be something that we should deal with, that question was lost and we all moved on to the next issue . . . I do not have a hidden agenda. If I'm correctly accused of one thing, it's being very open and very honest with people."

On capital punishment, Day said he would have a referendum and, yes, he does support it "in some cases. Whether you want to talk about serial killers or killers of children, there are some specific cases and with the added advantage now that we have with DNA, the opportunity to make a mistake is extremely remote."

After a few more questions on law and order, Mair asked Day, "Is homosexuality a sin?"

"Homosexuality is a choice, in my view," he said.

"They're not born with it?" asked Mair.

"I think there are a number of things and influences that go into our lives in any particular area, but ultimately what it comes down to is a matter of choice."

Mair asked if Day thinks homosexuals can be converted to heterosexuality. "No, . . . I don't think there is any role in government whatsoever in trying to convert people to anything . . . regardless of whether [people] choose to be celibate or whether they choose to be homosexual or heterosexual, I am a defender of human rights. I happen to agree with the present Liberal position that says marriage should be defined heterosexually." But he argued that Liberal amendments to Bill C-23, which extends pension benefits to homosexual couples, are "exclusionary and discriminatory. . . . We have many people in this country who are caring for another individual, be it a brother or a sister, an aging parent, or a young dependent adult, and to suggest that they should be barred from tax-supported support because they're not having sex with each other, I think we've missed the point here."

While Day was enroute to British Columbia before heading back to Red Deer the next day, his sister Rebecca Reynolds and her ten-year-old son Sam were piling into the family car in Grande Prairie, Alberta, heading off for what she describes as the "solid" seven-and-a-half-hour drive southeast to Red Deer to watch her big brother step up into federal politics.

Rebecca had told Sam's teacher she was taking him off to record a class project in civic affairs, and they brought along a video camera for the occasion. When the two finally arrived at the jam-packed Westerner Park pavilion, "All those people were there going wild over Stock. I thought, 'Wow, he's really come a long way from the days when he thought "All the Way with Stockwell Day" was a great campaign slogan.'"

Some fifteen hundred boisterous supporters showed up to cheer Day's official launch, a stark contrast to the modest 150 who had attended Manning's launch the day before. In his *Calgary Herald* column, Don Martin wrote: "The crowd was young, with blue jeans and baby carriages outnumbering suits and skirts. It was first and foremost a family affair featuring introductions by his sons, a summons onto the stage by his wife Val and music provided by an uncle. The signs were handpainted, the buttons proclaiming it's Day Time and the slogan a catchy call for Day to take The Next Step."

Setting aside the speech his officials had spent hours preparing, Day took dead aim at criminals and high-spending federal politicians, calling for "a justice system in which we give more respect to the rights of the victims than those who are causing the victims the hurt and the pain . . . It's time we fixed the parole system and dealt with truth in sentencing so when a judge says that's a life sentence, it doesn't mean — translated into Liberal jargon — a few years on the golf course."

His sharpest attack on the justice system was aimed at officials who allowed sex-killer Paul Bernardo to continue his appeals for freedom. He said Bernardo should be denied further appeals so the families of his victims can live in peace. He later told reporters he believes the majority of Canadians would support the death penalty for Bernardo.

"We need a rational and fair appeals process for every citizen . . . but I am sorry, ladies and gentlemen, when somebody has been videotaped committing atrocities . . . and they continue to be able to appeal and haunt and terrify and break the hearts of the families who lost their daughters at the hands of that horror, I'm sorry, I think the appeals should end at some point," he said to wild cheers.

Day said that Ottawa should be more aggressive in cutting the federal debt — a call greeted by a standing ovation — and called for specifically legislated debt pay-downs and mandated balanced budgets. In an attempt to distinguish himself from Manning, who has never been in government, Day said that his 14 years of government experience made him the best candidate to take the Alliance to power. Day also called for free votes and MP recall in the House. He mocked Chrétien's 37 years in power, comparing those years to "the same number of cents of every dollar that goes to servicing the Canadian debt."

He also lashed out at Chrétien over the Human Resources Development Canada job-grant controversy, saying, "When you put more money into golf courses and hotels in your old stomping ground that you do to the family farms in Alberta, I think your priorities are wrong."

Day said he has been trying for years to convince Ottawa to adopt Alberta's model of fiscal responsibility, but so far anyway, with little luck.

"I guess we'll just have to go to Ottawa and show them how it's done," he said.

9

THE RACE IS ON

Welcome to Ontario! Sort of.

Just hours after launching his official leadership campaign in Red Deer, Day hopped on a red-eye flight from Calgary to Toronto, made two early-morning television appearances, and then headed to an Internet café on Toronto's Bloor Street West to launch this country's first ever political e-mail polling system.

The importance of Ontario, of course, was not lost on any of the candidates or, for that matter, on the former Reform Party loyalists who voted 92 percent in favour of the Alliance. They voted largely in the hope that a Reform-Conservative coalition could achieve what Reform alone couldn't do — attract enough Ontario voters to win some seats.

While most of the people jammed into the café had come to praise Day, a group of nine protesters were there hoping to bury him, politically speaking. Chanting "Anti-choice, anti-gay, Stockwell Day, go away," these mouthy militants naturally received considerably more media attention than the large crowds who had come out to support him.

"We knew that was going to happen," says Day organizer Rod Love, Premier Ralph Klein's veteran strategist. "Nine people, the usual ragtag band of protesters, show up and make a lot of noise and the media reports that Stock's tour was ruined. We read the coverage. They said it was a disaster. There were a few protesters who disrupted the Web site. Is that a disaster? I don't think so. We think that people can see through that stuff."

They'd better hope so, because the major newspaper and broadcast coverage of Day's opening foray into Ontario demonstrated clearly — as Preston Manning also discovered when he first rode east to campaign in 1993 — that social conservatism guarantees a negative press.

There's no plot involved, no conspiracy. It's just that the vast majority of journalists are unabashed social liberals — although not liberal enough to tolerate a conservative viewpoint. Anybody advocating views that conflict with the accepted social orthodoxy is wrong at best and a flaming bigot at worst.

Hence the front-page headline on Manning's opening-day activities in Canada's largest newspaper, the *Toronto Star.* "What a Day! Alliance Hopeful Takes a Trip He'd Rather Forget."

Here's how the story begins: "It was a tough day for Stockwell Day. In his first day campaigning for the leadership of the Canadian Alliance, the former Alberta treasurer ran into noisy protesters, bad weather, tough questions from high school students and a visit to his Ontario childhood neighbourhood only to discover nobody seemed to remember him.

"To top it off, a new poll by Ekos Research Inc. places him far behind front-runner Preston Manning for the top job in Canada's newest political entity."

The *National Post,* picking up the same theme, declared "Ontario Electorate Fails to Follow Day's Game Plan." It makes it sound as if he should have caught the next plane back to Edmonton and pleaded with Klein for his old job back.

Was it really that bad a day? You be the judge.

He had two straightforward, nationally broadcast television interviews, and despite the tiny band of protesters, drew twice as many people to the Internet café as his organizers had anticipated.

He conceded — "under questioning" as the *Star* ominously put it — that "Health care is one of the single biggest concerns in the hearts of Canadians today and it has to be dealt with effectively."

As for the poll that placed him "far behind" Manning, as the *Star* put it, or said he "is not taken seriously" as a potential prime minister, as the *Post* put it — that came from a just-released Ekos poll in which respondents were read a list of seven names of prominent politicians and asked to "rate the degree to which they would be a good choice" for prime minister. Day finished last, at 16 percent. But that was before Day had even begun his campaign, and was actually just six points behind Manning, who had been a national leader since 1993. With a margin of error of 2.8 percentage points either way, in fact, those numbers could mean that the rivals were within a point or two of each other. What's more, Newfoundland Premier Brian Tobin (26 percent), Conservative leader Joe Clark (24), and Liberal Health Minister Allan Rock (20) didn't do much better. The only leaders who rated high marks were Prime Minister Jean Chrétien and Finance Minister Paul Martin, both with 48 percent.

In any event, after their morning in Toronto, the Day tour headed up Highway 400 to Barrie, some 90 minutes straight north of Toronto. There they found snow on the ground, which apparently accounts for the media references to "bad weather." Day may have been to blame for the snow, although snow in Barrie in March is about as unusual as — well, snow in Red Deer in March.

He briefly dropped by to visit the house that he moved from at age 2, some 47 years ago, which may explain why the neighbours didn't remember him. He lingered at a large maple tree in the backyard of the modest bungalow, saying, "This was my folks' first home. They paid $860 for it," then playfully tossed snowballs toward the house.

As Day made his way up the front steps to greet the homeowners, Bruna and Angelo Sanna, Bruna, 42, said, "This is the busiest the street has ever been." She's withholding judgement on both Day and the Alliance, although next-door neighbour Ken Keenan, 58, immediately bought an Alliance membership from Day. "I think we need something in this country," said Keenan. "Unless you vote Liberal, who else are you going to vote for? We can't have one party only."

Then it was off to a speech and question-and-answer session with high-school students at nearby Barrie Central Collegiate, were Day delivered his fiscal conservatism message. But the questions concentrated on his social conservatism. Grade 13 student Claire Woodside, the first up at the microphone, chided Day for his refusal to let homosexual couples become foster parents and for his vocal opposition to the Red Deer museum's use of a public grant to study the history of the town's homosexual community. "Do you feel this kind of homophobia is good for the country and follows your party's belief about [government] staying out of people's lives?" Day replied that his motive concerning homosexual foster or adoptive parents was in the best interest of children and that his opposition to the museum grant was responding to complaints from his constituents.

Ms. Woodside wasn't impressed — and that's fair enough. But Day knows, just as his leadership opponents do, that it is in medium-sized communities such as Barrie where the Alliance gospel of fiscal and social conservatism resonates the loudest in Ontario. Indeed, Barrie is at the heart of the only Ontario riding that Reform ever won. They lost it in 1997 after the riding was redistributed, but even then it was by less than four hundred votes.

Like it or not, however, Day — as well as Manning and Tom Long — have to expect a generally negative media response for their social conservatism in Ontario. As senior backroom federal Tory Peter White wrote, in a January 1999 opinion piece in the *National Post*, "Reform is perceived in some quarters as being anti-gay and anti-immigration, and not particularly welcoming to all religious and ethnic groups. Whether this is fair or not, as we all know, in politics perception is reality."

Rod Love, who has worked closely with Day for 11 years, says that Day "fights like hell in caucus for the views of the people who sent him there from Red Deer — and for his socially conservative views. But impose them on people? I've never seen it. When he loses, he loses. He just moves on. He never imposed his views on anybody. He could have, but he didn't.

"Listen, the best weapon we've got is Stockwell Day. That's why he's out on the road. To read the *Toronto Star* you'd think he was a knuckle-dragging, foaming-at-the-mouth nut. Yes, the media does cause problems, but the only way to get the real message out is you put Stockwell Day on the road. When people actually see him and hear what he has to say, they come away with a totally different image."

Day also recognizes the problem. Day spoke with me about a 20-minute scrum he experienced with journalists in Ottawa a few days later. "Once we got the first three or four predictable so-con questions out of the way, all the rest were on fiscal issues and changes to the democratic process. So what makes the nine-second sound bite? The so-con questions, of course, which makes it appear that all I'm doing is riding that horse, when in fact that's a very minor part of the message I'm trying to deliver."

What to do? "Either you don't talk about that stuff at all so it won't be reported, or you keep doing the interviews and hope that eventually your complete message will get through," says Day. "I've seen it all before. We got slagged with that every step of the way. When I went after my first nomination I got slagged. When I won I got slagged. Here's a guy coming into the legislature and he's going to impose church schools on everybody. But I stayed with my real message; I wasn't going to duck or hide. Now it's the national media doing exactly the same thing the local media did.

"I was in government 14 years, a good part of that in cabinet. I didn't bring in a law forcing everybody to go to church on Sunday or making Bible-reading mandatory on the streets of Edmonton.

"My experience has been with some people that if they only have the opportunity of viewing me through the media filter, yes, they have concerns. Once they meet me, that dissipates. They quickly learn that I deal in consensus. I respect the rights of other people to have different points of view. I'd like to enjoy the same rights for my views. I say, 'Here's our conflicting points of view. Some of these conflicts are irreconcilable. Now, how do we work within that reality to come to a workable understanding?' That's how I deal with it.

"No matter what business they're in, media or not, some people have difficulty in believing you can work side by side with somebody who you have profound disagreements with," says Day. "I've never had any difficulty doing that."

All the Alliance leadership candidates — and none would understand this better than Tom Long — can take comfort in the fact that right-wing Premier Mike Harris, although more a fiscal conservative than a social conservative, has been roasted in much of the media and plagued by massive protests since he was first elected. The final result of all that in good old "liberal" Ontario — Harris won more votes in his second majority victory than he did in the first, despite four years of uninterrupted festivals of indignation and assorted outrage from his political enemies.

The day after his visit to Barrie, Day was in London, Ontario. He appeared alongside Manning and Ontario junior minister Frank Klees on radio station CFPL's morning program. Day was asked about the nearly six hundred illegal Chinese immigrants who landed in rusting cargo ships on B.C.'s shores last summer. Expressing support for legal immigrants in Canada, and calling people who traffic in human smuggling "pirates," Day said, "First make sure they're healthy . . . cared for and given fresh clothes and medicine." He added that Canada should then pack them on a government Challenger jet, along with the minister of external affairs, and fly them all back to their home countries so they could fill in the proper paperwork. At the same time, the Minister could tell the foreign government that Ottawa would introduce sanctions if the refugee claimants were badly treated."

Questioned about the GST — since a proposal to axe the tax was voted down at the Alliance convention in January — Day at first said it needed to be "moderated." Later, he amended that to say it "needs to be reduced, with a longer-term hope to see it eliminated." Day was criticized by some for appearing to make serious economic policy on the fly, as he seemed to get tougher throughout the day on the question of eliminating the GST. He claims that, unlike Chrétien, he never promised to kill it, at least not right away, and his officials were griping at media reports that he was changing his policy as the day went on. But he was — he went from simply moderating it in the morning to reducing it and finally to eliminating it, albeit in the longer-term.

During its first week on the tour, the Day campaign sold more than eight hundred memberships. Campaign officials said that they must raise $100,000 a week in donations to stay out of debt during the three-month contest. Day usually travels with his wife, Val, known by the rest of the team as The Boss; campaign co-chair Jason Kenney; communications director Line Maheux; and, more often than not, his oldest son, Logan. For every public event, Day has two private ones, either to bring people onside or to get them to open their wallets, or both.

Norm Ovenden, of the *Edmonton Journal*'s Ottawa bureau, described a late-night drive from London to an overnight stop in Toronto before Day headed off for his first foray into Quebec. The team travelled along Highway 401 in two rented minivans with volunteer drivers, with all the interior lights on. "In one, the candidate read a prepared speech and struggled with pronunciations and upside-down syntax, hoping to brush up his rusty French." His handlers had ordered him to be disciplined, to resist his natural instinct to speak off the cuff and to stick to the text during an important campaign stop the following day in Montreal. The address being rehearsed was intended to prove that Day is the only contender for the Canadian Alliance leadership who can speak to Quebecers in both official languages.

In the other van, "Calgary MP Kenney, one of the new whiz-kids of

Canadian politics, had just found out that 10,000 sq. ft. of office space had been secured for a Calgary headquarters. Even better, it was free. . . ." At one point Kenney phoned Logan Day in the other minivan to remind him to make sure the candidate "knew the importance of the next day's early one-on-one encounter with a major fundraiser, a member of Premier Mike Harris's inner circle and the Ontario Conservative pipeline to Bay Street."

On March 30, Day ventured into Montreal with a speech before a small-business luncheon of about 50 people, pretty well sticking to the script. He sold himself as the champion of provincial powers and defender of the Constitution, attacking Ottawa for intruding too often into areas of provincial jurisdiction — a big issue in Quebec. "The fact that I talk about the Canadian Alliance and a prime minister that will respect the right of provinces, even as constituted now in the existing Constitution — that alone finds favour in the ears and minds of most Quebecers to whom I speak," he said. He skated around the issue of whether Quebec is a "distinct" society, saying, "There are many distinct features about Quebec . . . and there are also distinct elements with other provinces."

On the question of taxes, Day said provincial governments should collect all taxes above the local level and send Ottawa a cheque every year to sustain the federal administration. "This would shelter provinces from unilateral health and education cuts as ordered by the Chrétien government," he said. Day, who believes that a majority of 50 percent plus one would be sufficient for a referendum victory, offered cautious support of Chrétien's clarity bill. He also criticized it for not settling the issue of how a Quebec referendum question would be decided, or what majority would be required. On other significant details, such as the possibility of partition, Day took the advice of his handlers and avoided a direct response.

In early April came news that several of the architects of the Mike Harris "Common Sense Revolution," such as Tom Long, Alister Campbell, and Leslie Noble, were out to stage an Ontario coup of sorts. They planned to build a $3-million war chest by signing up 200,000 party members at ten dollars each, mostly from Ontario, through a direct-mail and tele-marketing drive. The funds would support the leadership campaign of their relatively obscure front man, Frank Klees, 49, a former gas company executive, financial consultant, and sports agent, who was a minister without portfolio in the Harris government.

The impetus from the Ontario Tories largely reflected what one senior Tory veteran called their "feverish fear," that in a head-to-head battle between Manning and Day, Manning would win. "Much of the talk in the meetings that I was involved with revolved around this concern. It's not necessarily personal. It's politics. Remember, these are people who are dedicated to beating the Liberals. They know Joe [Clark] can't do it. So that leaves the Alliance. And they're absolutely convinced, as I am, that Manning and Ontario don't match. As for Klees, he is hardly a household name. But they figure with their resources they can buy enough support to block a first-ballot Manning victory. That would allow them to go to Day on the second ballot. Not that they think he'll sweep Ontario either, but we all believe he could win enough seats to at the very least kill the Liberal majority."

Publicly, of course, Klees and his supporters were denying all that. Tom Long, who planned to run the Klees campaign, said, "If the western vote splits between Manning and Day, but we have this mountain of member-ships sold in Ontario, there's no reason why we can't win."

To make things worse for Joe Clark, Jim Jones, the only Conservative MP from Ontario, said publicly that the Alliance had "momentum" and that he would like the two parties to work together in his riding during the next election. "My goal is to run as a Conservative and have nobody to the right of me," he said, adding that the Alliance had awakened considerable interest in his constituency. "My constituents are going to take a look at it. They've decided it's time. They're tired of the Liberals. They want a small-c conservative government."

As excitement mounted through early April about Klees entering the race, and as the Alliance crowed that having an Ontario candidate in the race would add considerable credibility to the whole movement, a funny thing happened to Klees on the way to the podium.

On April 4, he stunned just about everybody by announcing that he wasn't going to run after all. Not only that, Klees said he was quitting because one financial backer pressured him to ally himself with another candidate after the first ballot, in return for a cash donation. "I refuse to participate and I refuse to accept those conditions," said Klees, adding he was "not prepared to compromise" his principles. Nor was he prepared to name names.

By quitting he way he did, Klees cast a pall of suspicion over both Manning and Day, both of whom quickly denied they had anything to do with a deal. Speculation centred more on Day than Manning, since it was no secret that the Ontario Tories would rather see Day as leader. Klees conceded that he had raised about $1.5 million, which is more than Day and Manning were spending. In the end, Klees ended up disgracing himself and annoying Tories and former Reformers alike. A senior Tory explained to me that "there were some strings with one donation. My information was it was for $400,000 and it was offered by a woman."

Tom Long, co-chair of the Klees campaign, hadn't matched his reputation as a master organizer with this botched effort to champion Klees. Long said at the time, "It's very disappointing. We'll just have to work twice as hard." As *Globe and Mail* columnist John Ibbitson wrote, "And Mr. Long, who has developed an aura of invincibility in the past two provincial elections, must grapple with the knowledge that he decided to back a candidate whom he couldn't even get out of the starting gate."

And so Long decided this time to back somebody he could trust — himself. While Klees began hinting that he might run after all, thanks to a groundswell of support for him, Long was quietly building his own campaign team. Finally, on Sunday, April 9, Klees called Long at home to tell him he was ready to announce his candidacy, only to be told that it was too late. Long was seeking the job himself.

Klees recalled, "I actually called Tom to let him know I . . . intended to get into the race this coming week, and it was during that telephone call that Tom advised me he was going to run. . . . I was probably more surprised than anyone else. . . . Do I feel disappointed? Of course." He also said he felt betrayed by Long, a hard-nosed fiscal and social conservative with considerable backroom experience, but none in elected office.

In a campaign stop in Sarnia in mid-April, Day, contrasting his electoral experience with Long's, made a point of stressing his experience on the front lines. "I put my record on the table, being the only one of the candidates who actually has a record of government service." That was the same day that the former Alberta treasurer was asked by *National Post* reporter Justine Hunter if he had ever smoked marijuana — she asked the question following a Day speech calling for tough laws against drug abuse — to which Day replied, "Yes, I have done marijuana and I did inhale. I haven't for about 30 years but, yes, I have." Ironically, the *Post* ran a little five-paragraph story on it well inside the paper, while the *Globe and Mail* published a huge colour picture of Day on the front page with a headline above saying, "I Did Inhale." It turned out to be one of Day's better days in the campaign.

After the news that Long was intending to run — he took his time making it official, basking in all the publicity while not having to answer questions from anyone — several senior Tories left their party and announced they were backing him. Arguably the most significant defection came on April 19, when Ontario's most powerful cabinet minister, Treasurer Ernie Eves, who had been a loyal Clark supporter and is Harris's best friend, announced he had quit the federal Conservatives to back Long's bid for the Alliance leadership. Eves, who had openly scorned the Alliance flat-tax proposal when it was approved as party policy, said for him the most important issue is for the Alliance to chose a leader who can rally everyone in Ontario who would vote for a small-c conservative party and defeat the Liberals.

"I don't see either Mr. Clark, whom I respect tremendously, or Mr. Manning, with whom I have no axe to grind, getting that job done," said

Eves. Although he did say that if Long doesn't win he would probably leave the Alliance, it is noteworthy that Eves did not mention Day when he said neither Clark nor Manning could rally Ontario small-c conservatives. Eves is definitely not a social conservative, but all he would say directly about Day is, "I know Stockwell a little bit, of course, because he has been a finance minister and has attended the odd finance ministers' meeting. I think he has done a fairly decent job in Alberta."

Eves did dismiss suggestions that Long was running to deprive Manning of a first-ballot victory and put Day in a position to win the second-ballot run-off. "I don't think Tom would be doing anything as a stalking horse for somebody else," he said. "I think the very thought of that would appal him." Perhaps — although it's hard to believe that Long and the other Ontario Tories really believed that Klees had a chance to win. Yet they were prepared to put their reputations on the line to run his campaign.

In the meantime, an Environics poll conducted between March 28 and April 16, after Reform had voted overwhelmingly to create the Alliance, showed Day was running well ahead in the West as the best choice for a new leader, preferred by 43 percent, compared to 30 percent for Manning. In Alberta, Day had the lead, with 50 percent over Manning's 18 percent. But in Ontario, Manning was slightly ahead, with 26 percent to Day's 20 percent. The poll of 2,020 adult Canadians did not include Long in its choices. It did, however, put BC MP Keith Martin as the best choice of 6 percent of respondents, the same support given to Klees, with Toronto lawyer Joe Peschisolido trailing at 2 percent.

Things got so desperate for the federal Tories that they turned to former prime minister Brian Mulroney, not the country's most popular politician, to help bail them out of their $7.4-million debt. Mulroney agreed to be the guest of honour at a $500-a-plate fundraising golf tournament and dinner on June 9 at the Angus Glen Golf Club in Markham, the area represented by Jim Jones. Despite Mulroney's support — it was his first attendance at such a political event since leaving office seven years ago —

even he has said he is open-minded about a new, right-wing alternative to the Liberals. He was quoted last year as telling friends that if Manning was replaced, he would look seriously at such an alternative.

No doubt it was thought that Mulroney's participation in the golf tournament would be a considerable draw for the Tory elite. But his emergence from retirement just two weeks before the Alliance vote could serve to underscore in the minds of some voters the connections and similarities between Mulroney and Long — not a partnership you'd particularly want to see on Long's dance card.

Both men were active in Conservative politics during their university days. Both became active backroom powerhouses, Mulroney in Quebec and Long in Ontario. And neither man had ever been elected when they went for the top prize. Mulroney missed in his first attempt in 1976, but won in 1983. There is no doubt that Long — who formally announced his candidacy on April 27 — like Mulroney years before, has built an impressive network of political operatives while working in the trenches. Both are lawyers, although Long, like Mulroney when he ran for the leadership, doesn't practice law. Mulroney was 37 during his first attempt and 44 when he won. Long entered his own race at 41.

In an April 24 column comparing the two men, the *Globe*'s veteran observer Hugh Winsor wrote that one big difference between them is that "Long is an ideologue wholly committed to minimalist government and more play to market forces" while Mulroney "was never ideologically driven. . . ." Mulroney had considerably more business experience, too, as counsel to a landmark commission of inquiry into construction violence in Quebec and as president of the Iron Ore Company of Canada.

"Long has been a political organizer, speechwriter and executive-search consultant," wrote Winsor. Another key difference he didn't mention was that while Long is unilingual in English, Mulroney has a perfect command of both English and French.

When Peter White took over Brian Mulroney's patronage machine in 1984, he hired Tom Long as his assistant. One of the complaints that

Mulroney and others had made about Clark's leadership was that he hadn't rewarded enough of his Tory loyalists, a warning White and Long apparently took to heart. Senator Marjory LeBreton, who took over the job after they departed, told *Toronto Star* columnist Ian Urquhart the two men "carried their mandate to extremes." She found files littered with "pejorative remarks" about potential appointees, including notations about which ones had supported Clark for leader.

Urquhart also quotes the highly respected Charles McMillan, Mulroney's senior policy adviser, as he recalled a dinner in Hull, Quebec, after the 1984 election, with White, Long, and others in attendance. When the discussion turned to the role of ideology in politics, says McMillan, Long was befuddled by suggestions that the regional nature of Canadian politics might conflict with any ideological agenda. He said the unilingual Long "had no feel for Quebec, or, for that matter, for the Maritimes or the West. Regional concerns meant the square root of nothing for Tom."

That Urquhart feature on Long also underscores another concern that social conservatives have felt about Long. During his term as president of the Ontario Tories in the mid 1980s, Long fervently preached the gospel of "family values" that is so important to so many Reform/Alliance supporters, then and now. Yet he was quoted at the time as saying, "My little girl came home the other night and she'd got her orange badge in swimming. I didn't even know she was taking swimming lessons." There were also whispers about an affair. Gina Brannan, a red Tory who served on the party executive with Long, came across him embracing Leslie Pace on the street and asked, "Is this what family values are all about, Tom?" Long subsequently left his wife and married Pace.

One of the more intriguing but underreported aspects of the current campaign, in fact, is that while Day took considerable heat during the first week for his socially conservative views, Manning and then Long made a point of underscoring their own social conservatism, yet the media hasn't gone after them with a vengeance. In Manning's case, perhaps it's because he had already endured those attacks on his "intolerance" from the assembled champions of tolerance, who make a point of tolerating everything they personally agree with, but little else.

Manning, who was legitimately criticized by many Reform supporters for soft-pedalling his social views in the Commons, said near the beginning of the campaign that people shouldn't expect to hear much difference in social views. "My views would be comparable to Mr. Day's in a number of those areas, and there's millions of other people who share them," he said. And Long, in his formal leadership announcement, said that he too opposes abortion and favours a national referendum on both that issue and capital punishment (which he opposes). He also said that he believes the family is a heterosexual institution and that he would like to see more private-sector money put into the health-care system.

Why would these men be making these points if social conservatism would hurt them with potential Alliance voters? "Because it helps them," says one senior Tory official who has had access to internal party polling. "You would think from reading the newspapers that these ideas are the domain of three Neanderthals living in a cave somewhere in northern Alberta. In fact, among the kind of people who would be most likely to vote for the Alliance, socially conservative views represent a huge segment of their constituency. There are varying degrees, of course, but overall those that hold to social conservatism represent a healthy majority. Don't tell him I said this, but that's something that Joe [Clark] never understood, and it's hurt him. Not that he should have pretended he agreed with them, but he could have been less dismissive."

On this score, Long has never really been publicly tested. Day has at least walked the walk, standing firm in the face of some pretty heavy artillery fire. When Manning was faced with controversial comments from some of his own Reform MPs, who made what were widely seen as anti-homosexual remarks, he buckled under the pressure and penalized them. To hard-core social conservatives such as Link Byfield, publisher of *Alberta Report*, that's when Manning "lost his lustre. You'd never see Stock openly kick his own supporters in the head. You may disappoint your own core, but you don't want to insult them. Manning buckled to this militant secularism. Burn a little incense here. You really have to piss on the Christians. What he was really saying is we don't want Judeo-Christian conservatives in our party. He painted them as extremists. Stock won't do that. Everybody understands you've got to stay as close to the middle as you can sometimes, but as long as the cock crows three times and he's not denying us as Manning did, Stock will get that kind of support."

During April, in the wake of a number of high-profile desertions from his party to the Alliance — particularly to the Long camp — Clark admitted that his party was losing ground and hinted he might try to get a seat in the Commons to increase his profile. "If there is a riding that seems attractive or open or possible, then certainly it might be more useful for me to be in the House of Commons," he said.

Clark was nominated as the Tory candidate in Calgary Centre, where just about everybody agreed on his slim chances of winning. In Nova Scotia, Cumberland-Colchester Tory MP Bill Casey, considering retirement before the next election, made it clear he'd be willing to step aside and leave a safe Tory seat open for Clark to win in a by-election. Clark had already declined six times to run in by-elections since winning the party's leadership, and his party had lost more than 88,000 paid-up members. A few days after hinting he was thinking of running, he announced that he had changed his mind.

As for Day, he kept up his frantic pace, and was by far the most visible of all the candidates. In one 24-hour stretch in April, for example, he delivered three separate speeches, all with question-and-answer periods, did two television interviews, and made appearances in five different communities stretching from Toronto to Sarnia. On April 13, 36 members of Ralph Klein's Alberta Tory caucus pledged their support to Day. Calgary Northwest MLA Greg Melchin said, "We have all known Stockwell during his time as an MLA, and during his times as Minister of Labour, Minister of Family and Social Services and Provincial Treasurer. We support both him and the future of the Canadian Alliance as Canada's true small-c conservative party." Day said he was "both humbled and honoured by their support."

One neighbouring politician who wasn't supporting him was Red Deer Reform MP Bob Mills, a Manning supporter. "I've been through a lot with Preston right from the beginning. I have a loyalty to him that's much deeper than anything else to me. Preston is the smartest guy I've ever worked with. His big problem is that he lacks that TV charisma. Stock certainly has that. Preston is much more reserved and more laid-back and that's sometimes not a plus in politics, but Preston has come out looking more like a statesman.

"Stock has done an excellent job as an MLA. People like him. He's supported me in the last two elections. His wife is a real gem. So he has a lot going for him. But Stock has to learn a lot. Federal politics is a lot different than provincial politics, but he's done an excellent job as treasurer," said Mills. " I can't say anything negative about him."

He hasn't always said positive things either. Mills almost won provincially in Red Deer in 1979 as a Social Credit candidate and finished second as an independent in 1982. During Day's inaugural campaign in 1986, the closing days were a tight battle against Liberal Don Campbell. Mills likened the Day-Campbell contest to a recent hockey series between the defending Stanley Cup champion Edmonton Oilers and the underdog Calgary Flames, who had just pulled a major upset by beating the Oilers. "Who would have put money on the Flames? But they worked hard," he said. "I would call Don Campbell the Flames."

In a *Globe and Mail* interview in April, Day said there would be few policy differences among the candidates. "The differences that people are looking for are track record — what have you done — and the ability to communicate — one on one, with groups or over the airwaves."

He didn't mention Manning by name, but he said, "People want to feel that the person is reaching out to them. Reaching out, and listening, and then able to do something with what they say."

Reaching out to people in a personal way has consistently been a problem for the more cerebral Manning. Link Byfield tells the story of a close friend of his who spent a whole evening at a political event in Calgary sitting at a roundtable with Manning and ten other people. "Preston didn't ask him his name or chat him up for the whole evening. He's all process and abstractions. Anybody else hustling votes for a living would know who he was and who everybody else at the table was, and what they do for a living, all that small talk that is important to people. This comes easily for Stock. I know it's an odd thing to say, but Manning isn't a politician. Politicians are the way they are for a reason. There has to be a sense among people they actually give ashit about me as a person. If you're bloodless and analytical and show no personal warmth — well, you're not going to get that far."

Day kept up his hectic campaign schedule, appearing at a leadership candidates' forum in Burnaby, B.C., along with Martin and Peschisolido, before seven hundred people at the glitzy new Hilton Hotel. Long, who still hadn't formally launched his campaign at that point, wasn't there. Neither was Manning. About Long, Day said, "It will be exciting to have another Ontario candidate." On Manning's absence, he simply stated, "I like a full race but everyone has to account for themselves."

The next day he outlined a tough law-and-order program to an appreciative audience of two hundred people in Abbotsford, about 60 kilometres east of Vancouver, in the riding of Alliance justice critic Randy White. Day called for work camps for young criminals, longer prison sentences for repeat offenders of all ages, and harsh penalties for people-smugglers. He criticized what he called a "dishonest, soft-on-crime approach" to offenders. "I believe that Canadians are no longer prepared to sit back and watch the interests of offenders dominate their criminal justice system, and outweigh the rights of victims."

He also called for sweeping changes to the Young Offenders Act to require anyone over 15 accused of a violent crime or repeat offence to be tried in adult court. Day would also scrap the current policy of mandatory release after two-thirds of a sentence is served, and replace it with "discretionary parole" that would be earned through good behaviour.

While most of the emphasis on the leadership campaign played out in the West and Central Canada, all the candidates, Day included, attempted to mine whatever support they could find in Atlantic Canada as well. The East Coast is an area of the country that has not been receptive to their notions of a minimal government role in the economy.

When Day rolled into Halifax on March 31, for instance, about ten members of the International Socialists and the Canadian Federation of Students tried to force their way into the Holiday Inn meeting room, where about a hundred Alliance supporters, twice what they had expected, were gathered to hear him speak. While they chanted, "Racist, sexist, anti-gay, Stockwell Day, go away," Day arrived at the hotel and casually strode by the protesters without incident — they didn't even recognize him. In his speech, Day stuck to his mantra of debt reduction, tax relief, and more free votes in Parliament, but aimed much of his message at the Progressive Conservatives in the audience, including three Tory MLAs: Tim Olive, David Hendsbee, and Brooke Taylor. "I want to say to federal and provincial Tories, I know the emotion of working for years for a party I believed in," he said. "But I had to ask myself . . . should we cling emotionally to that which is in the past, or should we reach out to what could be in the future?" Day also mentioned he had lived in New Glasgow as a young child, and quoted Charles Tupper's ideas on federalism to give his speech a local flavour.

If people think Clark's problems in Ontario and the West are hurtful, they pale by comparison to the potential drainage of federal Tory support in the East. After all, of the 20 seats the Tories won in the 1997 federal election, 13 of them were in Atlantic Canada. Since then, they've gained one, when New Brunswick New Democrat Angela Vautour crossed the floor, but they lost a seat when Newfoundland's Bill Matthews bolted the party to join the Liberals. Another Tory concern during the Alliance leadership race was a by-election to keep the Newfoundland seat vacated by

Charlie Power, no fan of Clark's leadership.

That's why Nova Scotia Tories were jolted by the events of late April. Clark had just suffered another serious blow when Quebec Tory MP André Harvey, the party's whip, left the Tories to sit as an independent. Then Nova Scotia's Conservative Party president, Tom Jarmyn, announced he was leaving the party to join the Alliance and work on Long's campaign.

Stephen Greene, who ran unsuccessfully for Reform in Halifax against NDP Leader Alexa McDonough, then worked as Manning's chief of staff in Ottawa after the 1993 election, said the best Reform ever did in Nova Scotia was about 18 percent of the vote. But Greene, who conducts informal party polls in the region, says he thought Manning would win about half the delegate votes in Nova Scotia, with Day at 30 percent and Long with 20 percent. He added that Day would do much better in New Brunswick. "They're far more socially conservative in New Brunswick than they are in Nova Scotia."

Greene says there are two kinds of Reformers in Nova Scotia. "We're all fiscal conservatives, and then we're either libertarian or social conservatives. The social conservatives are a bit frustrated with Preston Manning. Although he himself has those views, he's very carefully been able to reach across and soften the perception. Day, it seems to me, has given people who have strong social conservative views a new voice. In this part of the country, loyalty is a big thing. A lot of people, even if they have concerns about Preston, have an innate loyalty to him. On the other hand, a lot feel he's gone as far as he can go. There is a substantial body of opinion in Atlantic Canada who feel that way. A lot of those people will go with Day and others will go with Long."

MLA Brooke Taylor, Nova Scotia's deputy speaker, who flirted briefly with running federally for Reform, says, "the ties that bind the federal PCs and the provincial PCs together are tightly wound here. But I have noticed since Mr. Day came on the scene there is a slight loosening of those tight knots. There comes a time when you realize the status quo won't cut it any more. For us blue Tories, I was quite disheartened when I heard that a federal New Democrat quit to join Mr. Clark's Tories. It makes us very concerned about the direction he has taken the party.

"A lot of people are looking for leadership and guidance. There are a lot of 'closet' Alliance supporters here, even in our own caucus. Day was received warmly here. He didn't push his personal views on abortion and homosexuality. It doesn't bother me that we differ on some of those issues because we agree on the things that are more important to me and my own constituents, who are interested in lower taxes, law and order, and strengthening democratic accountability. The Alliance is more in tune with those issues than the federal PCs are."

This parallels what many capital-C Conservatives have been saying right across the country, which is obviously the point of the whole exercise, regardless of who ultimately wins the leadership race.

EPILOGUE

—

Readers of the *Globe and Mail* must have been shocked on April 22, 2000, to learn that an Angus Reid survey of 1,500 adult Canadians for the *Globe* and CTV found that 84 percent of respondents said, yes, they do believe in God.

Eighty-four percent! Perhaps Godless Canada is not so godless after all.

What's more, 69 percent believe that through the life, death, and resurrection of Jesus, God provided a way for the forgiveness of sins, 67 percent said their religious faith is very important to their day-to-day life, and 66 percent believe the Bible is the inspired word of God.

Angus Reid's senior vice-president, Andrew Grenville, said he wasn't surprised that so few young Canadians regularly attend church, since only about 20 percent of all adult Canadians do. But, he added "in some ways . . . [it] is astonishing" that so many young Canadians, who did not grow up in the institutional church as so many of their parents had, have retained their faith.

This no doubt will come as bad news to the champions of militant secularism, so many of whom are journalists who have made a career of mocking those who publicly admit to faith in God.

Of all the criticisms levelled at Stockwell Day during the leadership race, none is more persistent than the charge that Day, by virtue of his avowed Christian faith, is a dangerous man who wants to impose his "narrow" views on the rest of us.

Preston Manning suffered through these same vicious attacks when he came east in 1993, mostly from people who claimed to be the champions of tolerance, but who only tolerate their own vision of a secular society, where religion — or more to the point, faith — has no place in politics. The viciousness of the attacks — unsubstantiated charges of racism, bigotry, and all the rest — eventually cowed Manning, certainly not into abandoning his faith, at least into depositing it for safekeeping outside of the political arena.

Shortly after Day officially entered the race, *Globe* columnist Jeffrey Simpson reflected the view of most journalists — and certainly of Day's critics — in a column entitled, "Leave the Prayer Book at Home, Stockwell." Simpson wrote: "That Mr. Day has strong religious beliefs is fine; that he brings them into the public domain is not. At least not in this secular country."

But are we really a secular country? I think not. My dictionary defines secularism as belief "in a system of political or social philosophy that rejects all forms of religious faith and worship." With so many Canadians believing in God, and so many saying their faith is important to them on a day-to-day basis, perhaps all those religion bashers or faith haters — to borrow some terms from the great social liberals — should look in the mirror and see where intolerance begins and ends. Or, as *National Post* columnist Mark Steyn put it, "Under the new intolerant 'tolerance,' expressions of moral traditionalism must be driven from public life."

I am not a member of the Canadian Alliance and have no intention of becoming one. That's because I have no intention of joining anything, preferring instead a life of drifting around outside looking in, rather than being inside and having to tailor my views and actions on behalf of one group or another.

But if I were a voting member of the Canadian Alliance, I would vote for Stockwell Day.

I may be disappointed in the end. He is, after all, a politician. But in nearly 40 years of writing about politicians, I've never seen one as open and transparent as he is. Yes, he sometimes says dumb things, but then what politician doesn't? Jean Chrétien? Joe Clark? Who?

Of the major candidates, he is the only one who can speak and be spoken to in French. Not that I would know, but those who do say his French is rusty — he never claimed it wasn't — but good enough that he would soon be quite fluent should he have to live in the nation's capital and deal regularly with both official languages.

While the Reform Party under Manning attracted nothing but hostility in Quebec — particularly with the 1997 election campaign ads showing lines through the faces of Quebec politicians — Day's fluency in French and his support of provincial powers prompted five prominent political veterans to write an open letter endorsing Day. The letter, which earned front-page coverage in *Le Devoir,* was signed by André Tremblay, a former consitutional adviser to Robert Bourassa; Jean Allaire, founder of the Action démocratique du Québec party; Denis Hardy and Gérard Latulippe, former Bourassa cabinet ministers; and Michel Rivard, a former Parti Québécois MNA. Such public support is obviously helpful in Quebec itself, and while it is generally not seen as a major factor in western Canada, it is also an advantage in gaining support among significant elements of the voting public in both Ontario and New Brunswick, Quebec's next-door neighbours.

Day was also competent enough in French to appear on radio with Gilles Proulx, the feisty and unpredictable host of a popular Montreal midday program on CKAC, an act considered risky even for veteran Quebec politicians. And with the final of three leadership debates slated for Montreal on June 12, Day will be the only candidate able to debate in French. This is a point not lost even on supporters of the other hopefuls. When Long announced, for example, that he'd been endorsed by Jonathan Sauvé, former president of the Quebec Liberal youth wing, Sauvé said that Long was committed to learning the language. But he conceded that Long's inability to speak French is a problem. "I can't imagine a prime minister not being able to speak to up to 25 percent of the population."

Another significant advantage that Day has over his two main rivals is that he is the only leadership hopeful with real practical experience in governing, as opposed to either bitching from the sidelines about what the other guys are doing, or manipulating from the backrooms while somebody else faces the music.

Preston Manning is a fine, sincere man — a bit autocratic at times, but exceptionally honest for somebody in his chosen field. But he cannot win in Ontario, which is one of the reasons why only half of those who know him best — his caucus — are supporting him. He says he can win Ontario, but 1993 and 1997 say otherwise. He's demonstrated his weakness in Ontario — twice. And without at least 15 or 20 seats in Ontario, all Manning's efforts to spread the gospel of conservatism to the East will fall short once again.

Tom Long has certainly attracted a large number of high-profile Conservatives to his cause, especially in the key battleground of Ontario. But most of them appear to be simply on loan, with no genuine commitment to anything other than helping the Ontario contingent stage a coup, or at least control who does win, since so many have said they wouldn't stay with the Alliance if Long doesn't win.

Long is the only candidate, as Conservative activist Geoff Norquay put it on a CBC Newsworld panel, "with his own national newspaper [the *Post*]," which makes it difficult to know the answer to the question *Toronto Star* columnist Thomas Walkom recently posed: "Is Tom Long making the news or is the news making Tom Long?" Long is certainly a bright, talented man. He's the kind of person who was born into the political game, but he is one of those bloodless operatives who see the game not only as the thing, but as the only thing.

In one headline in the *Post*, Long was described as a moderate. If he's moderate, then Toronto Maple Leafs feisty forward Tie Domi is this year's winner of the Lady Byng Trophy for gentlemanly conduct on the ice. It is, I suspect, because of Long's unbridled toughness, his unflinching ideological confidence, that a former Conservative leader named Brian Mulroney was so attracted to him almost 20 years ago.

British Columbia MP Keith Martin, a 39-year-old physician, is widely described as a moderate within the party because he is pro-choice, but he is also the only candidate — and perhaps the only politician in the country — openly campaigning for a two-tier, private/public health-care system. I think he's right, but he's ahead of his time. Medicare is so ingrained in the Canadian psyche that it will have to become a lot worse than it is right now before the country is ready to embrace a British-style health system.

As this is being written, the deadline for leadership candidates to pony up their $25,000 refundable deposits and lists of three hundred supporters is still a month away, so it's not certain how many candidates will actually appear on the June 24 ballot.

Manning, Day, and Long are the only three official candidates at the moment. Martin is expected to be on the ballot, but he hasn't made it official yet. Toronto lawyer Joe Peschisolido announced he was dropping out of the race in order to support Long. There are two other candidates, or at least two other people who claim to be candidates: Margaret Kopala, an Ottawa writer, community activist, and failed federal Tory candidate from 1997; and John Long, a Formosa, Ontario, businessman.

As things stand now, it is highly unlikely that any of the big three — Manning, Day, and Long — can win it on the first ballot. This puts Day in a strong position, since he would be a more palatable second choice for the Manning people — who don't like the notion of an Ontario coup — and similarly more acceptable as a second choice for the Long people — who believe, as I do, that Manning can't win in Ontario and that a "new" party with the "old" leader is the same old party.

There are other reasons to think that Day is on to something here. Several times during the campaign, Manning made a point of saying that he is just as socially conservative as Day. Why would he say that if being socially conservative was political suicide? They have polls. All parties do. And why would Long, a fervent fiscal conservative to be sure, go out of his way to underscore his opposition to abortion and call for a referendum on capital punishment? And why doesn't that make Long extreme?

But the real proof that Day is Alliance's biggest threat to the sitting Liberals came from the Liberals themselves. At their raucous convention last March, when the forces of Paul Martin attacked the forces of Jean Chrétien, and lost, Day's impending candidacy was on everybody's lips.

Chrétien himself, in his otherwise un-noteworthy keynote drone — er, speech — said this: "We don't want a party that is very much in the hands of the fundamentalists of the right."

"Fundamentalists," of course, is code for Day. Or, as Paul Adams wrote in the *Globe,* "Some of [the Liberals] say they find Mr. Day 'scary,' and they mean it in a double sense; they fear he represents the voice of intolerance and they worry he could catch fire politically."

They should worry.

INDEX

—